M000207914

The Midnight Midwife

Annelisa Christensen

The Midnight Midwife
Published 2019 by Dustie Books

Copyright © 2019 Annelisa Christensen
The moral right of Annelisa Christensen to be identified as author of this work has been asserted in accordance with the Copyright, Designs and Patents Act 1988.

All rights reserved. *The Midnight Midwife* is copyright material and must not be copied, reproduced, transferred, distributed, leased, licensed or publicly performed or used in any way except as specifically permitted in writing by the publisher, as allowed under the terms and conditions under which they were purchased or as strictly permitted by applicable copyright law. Any unauthorized distribution or use of this text may be a direct infringement of the author's and publisher's rights, and those responsible may be liable in law accordingly.

ISBN: 978-1-9998173-7-4 (e)
ISBN: 978-1-9998173-8-1 (paperback)
ISBN: 978-1-9160877-0-5 (large print)

Cover by Jesh Art Studio
(based on a concept by Carmen Christensen)

Formatting for paperback by Timothy Savage
timsavagewrites.com

Reach author Annelisa Christensen online:
www.annelisachristensen.com
twitter.com/Alpha_Annelisa
www.scriptalchemy.com/
www.facebook.com/scriptalchemy

The Midnight Midwife

ANNELISA CHRISTENSEN

Table of Contents

To my sisters, Karen and Helen,
my lifelong friends.

We can distinguish the common human nature
from that which is peculiar, and therefore wonderful.

-Saint Aurelius Augustine (Bishop of Hippo) 354-430 AD

1

Market Day

'I'll take a dozen to collect later.'

Without answering, the chandler, thin and rancid-smelling as his candles, wrapped the tallow sticks around the middle with brown paper and neatly tied the bundle with a length of rough string.

I tried again. 'It seems Madam Spring sweeps Old Man Winter from our doorstep.'

He nodded but still did not speak. Not wishing for him to ruin my mood, I paid, bid him good day and placed the candles in my basket as I moved along to the next stall.

Only then did I notice my daughters had not followed me and dallied some paces behind at the milliner's stall. The shop-keeper, encouraged by the warm spring sun and lack of wind, had displayed his wares outside and my girls, infused with good humour and high spirits, tried first one then another of the most splendid bonnets on display.

I smiled and called to them. 'Come along girls. We do not have all day for the market if we are to have our picnic as well.' But they were unmindful of anything but their business at hand, and so I returned to them, not failing to notice how striking they appeared together.

Mary, the tallest, was as a red flag on the battlefield of market day, her height drawing attention to the three of them. Her stature was greatly tempered by the smallest of waists, making it unnecessary for her to use a tight corset although, wishing to be in the latest style, she wore one nevertheless. It did not achieve everything she desired in that it did not give her the fullness of breast where none was to be found, but the scarf around her neck and shoulders cleverly hid any lack. As for her hair, where she wore her chestnut dress tight, she wore her curled brown tresses loose, resembling, but not moulding to, modern taste.

Only when one came close enough to see her rare blue eyes was all else about her face made drab. Rare laughter caught at their corners and wrung the shine from her lashes as she and Elin teased young Judith with two hats held out of reach. Then did the beauty in those eyes arrest me. I thought of Cornflowers, as I so often did whenever I caught sight of them.

If Mary was tall and elegant, Elin was formed in a more homely mould, with curves softening every bone. Most of her hair was pulled back beneath her bonnet, leaving two fashionable long ringlets to frame her gentle cheeks until she turned and they swung across her face. She was the envy of her sisters, for she was blessed not only with good complexion but also ample mounds above her corset. A picture of rude health, she waved the blue flower-laced bonnet at Judith.

Then there was my youngest daughter, Judith, preparing for, but not yet ready to embark upon, the trials of womanhood. In my eyes, she looked unlike either of her sisters though in her dress and hair their guiding influence was obvious. Her dress followed the simple lines of Mary's, for my eldest always did have a better eye for design than most others. And her hair was lovingly brushed and dressed by Elin, who preferred those touches of social grace given a young woman by the more practiced worldliness of an older one.

'You cannot have it both ways,' said Elin.

'But why ever not, I ask you?' Judith lept, grabbed both colourful pieces of fabric and spun on her toes holding them out before her, the long ties twisting round her arms like ribbons on a maypole. 'If I am divided on which is the better, and the benefits of both are of equal value, why can I not choose both?'

Mary laughed, and again I took satisfaction in her changed mood, congratulating myself on the success of my scheme. 'I can tell you a reason why you should take care to come down on one side or another, though you must suffer my story patiently, for it is not about bonnets.'

'A story?' Without thinking, one in each hand, Judith squeezed the two bits of fabric as she pressed her hands together with pleasure. 'Amuse us, Mary, do!'

'Can you recall the mayor caught between two armies in the war?' Mary spoke plainly, but we all of us knew she would embellish with voice and actions once we were caught in curiosity.

'She will not recall that history, I am certain.' Elin answered before Judith was able. 'She is too young to remember old Mr Clarke that told it to us.'

'Then shall I relate it as well as I remember.' Mary picked up a straw bonnet, inspected it and placed it back on the stall. As she turned back around, holding her arm across her face pretending it held a cloak, she peered deep into each of us with great intensity and seriousness of a storyteller and spoke with far-reaching voice to suit the stage.

"Twas during the civil war, this story be told. The Roundheads on one side and the Cavaliers on the other. One day, on a day far more bitter than today, when flesh-eating wind howled and the rain burned like knives through men's armour, then into town from the north came the drumming of the King's hardy men, marching forth to do battle.' Mary turned to the north, placed her hand on her forehead as if shielding her eyes from the sun and pointed. Then, swinging her leg around she turned on her other foot into the opposite direction and cupped her ear with her hand. 'And, hark! What is that? Tis the horn of Cromwell's powerful army marching through the streets from the south. And there!' She pointed at the Meeting Hall with her whole arm. 'Right in the middle of town, between the two armies, the poor mayor and his council, that had no part of either side, found themselves in a fearful predicament!'

'What happened then, girl?' Others in the market had stopped at a distance to listen to a well-told story, their curiosity allowing them to speak out. Mary took on a devilish face, and played up to them as well as her sisters, becoming more solemn and frowning deeply.

'There in the Meeting Hall they sat, trapped between the two ferocious armies, the quaking mayor and his trembling men, all heads bowed together, not knowing whom they should welcome. Their plight could not have been less plain. If they should welcome Cromwell's men and the King's Cavaliers were victorious, they would bring down upon them the ire of the King. And if they should greet the King's men and then the roundheads raised their flag, they would likewise find themselves in trouble with the victor.' Shoulders raised, Mary held her arms wide in question, then spoke in a deeper, more confiding voice.

'The mayor asked, 'What should I do? What should I do?' No matter which army they welcomed, they were certain to wrong-foot the other. Do you know what he did then?' Though Mary did not address them, some bystanders shook their heads, but not Elin. She opened her mouth to answer. 'No, Elin. You must not spoil my story.' She held one finger to her own lips, the other to Elin's. Her wink made light of her order. Elin smiled behind the finger. 'So, can you guess, Judith?'

'I cannot. Tell me, do!'

As always, Judith was entranced by her eldest sister. Adoringly, she looked up a good hand span into the older girl's teasing face and shook her head. But she was not to be satisfied with the rest of the story straight away. I smiled. Mary did so enjoy provoking the younger ones. She pretended to see something of great interest and distraction to herself on the other side of the stall.

'Oh, see here! This would be simply perfect for you, Mother.'

'Aye, the colour will suit me quite well.' In an equally light mood, I was inclined to get up on the same pony and ride along with her tease. I took the large, blue hat trimmed with English lace and tried it on. Then I moved my head up and down, trying to catch a glimpse of the bonnet in the many small facets of the milliner's shop window, each laced with dust in the corners and each facing a slightly different direction. Like a broken looking glass, it divided the world into many little reflections.

Various of the small square window panes showed fragments of a sham-market imitating the bustle behind us. In that backward world, visitors to the town stopped to buy meat, fish, wool, eggs, fabric, building nails, baskets, leather goods, pots and pans, medicines and potions and every other manner of thing one could imagine.

Regular sellers displayed their wares on a stall, others laid them in pots or baskets on the ground, while those that owned a shop around the edge of the market-place lowered the whole of their wooden shop front to the ground and used it as a large table with their goods of trade set upon it. This also had the benefit of allowing us to see them hard at work inside.

In that pane there, a pedlar bartered a fish for a rabbit, two loaves of bread or vegetables for a stew. And in that pane, a farmer secreted his beasts to the pens to avoid being chastised by the aldermen for his late arrival. He should have had them where they belonged by dawn. In contrast to the broken colours and the bustle of the market, yet other panes faced the sky and showed glimpses of pale blue stillness. But above all others in importance were the many reflections of my daughters and myself indulging ourselves in a little gaiety together.

Then my eyes saw themselves.

Though memory would convince me I resembled Mary in face and figure as once I did, I was deceived by it. Indeed, my reflection worked heartily to be disagreeable and show me otherwise.

I had forgotten the lines that now made fences around every feature. Those around the mouth revealed how laughter had in later years outweighed the tears, but those around my eyes only worsened the dark shadows of the past beneath them. And even the rippled glass could not disguise the shine of grey around my temples that might distinguish an alderman but age a woman, nor or a waist unbound by young flesh.

'The colour does not suit after all,' I said.

I pulled off the bonnet, carelessly loosening one of my hairpins, and handed it back to Mary. Perhaps the bonnet would have delighted me twenty years past, but now it merely reminded me I was the mother not the child. I righted my dishevelled hair.

'You are right, mother.' Mary removed the bonnet she had been trying and replaced it with the one I had discarded. It was a delight, the colour emphasising her striking blue eyes and her smooth angular cheeks that reminded me of perhaps Egyptian or Eastern origins, but mostly the ghost of my younger self. 'This one would be the perfect addition to my own wardrobe!'

'Mary! Do not tease me so!' Judith pouted and her eyebrows tried to meet in the middle.

Mary pretended to remember that she was telling the story, but did nothing to cloak her triumph that Judith hung onto her every word. She returned to the tale in no louder than a gruff whisper that we had to still ourselves to hear.

'Ah, the poor mayor. Yes, he had a most difficult decision. But this mayor, he considered himself a cunning man and devised a crafty design.' Mary paused for effect, and even I and Elin, who had heard the story before, held our breath so we could better hear Mary's next words. But we need not for she became louder as she spoke. 'Indeed, the town's elders hailed him as a hero. He wrote one scroll of welcome to the leader of the Roundheads and another to the leader of the Cavaliers. Then, not knowing who had won the battle, he went boldly forth to meet the victor, confident he was wholly prepared with one scroll placed in each of his sleeve pockets. I expect you are commending the mayor on being so clever, but what do you think happened then?'

I heard a murmur from one or two of the men and women who had gathered to listen nearby. They knew the answer. I too knew the answer and happily awaited the end of the tale, but the suspense was all too much for Elin. She laughed and twice clapped her hands. 'He gave him the wrong scroll!'

Instead of being cross with Elin for stealing her show, Mary only laughed at Elin's excitement and finished, 'Alas. Instead of appeasing the leader of the incoming army, he only angered him!'

'Did they... did they have his head?' Judith, enthralled by her sisters, grinned at first one and then the other.

'They should have, the fool.' I said my piece. 'I do not know how he talked the victor into only casting him into prison.'

'And that, my dear Judy, is why you should not sit undecided in the middle,' said Mary.

A few of those that had stayed to listen clapped. Mary bowed and they went on their way.

Judith, the frown now completely gone, pouted once more at her sisters' good natured tease and said hats were hardly like armies.

'Mrs Harris!' I ignored the woman's loud, shrill voice. 'Abigale!'

I sighed. And there, it seemed, alas, was my own predicament. Mrs Brown.

Before turning to greet the baker's wife, I cleared the exasperation I knew must be in my face.

'Over here, Mrs Harris!' She waved at me.

I could avoid her no longer.

2

𝕬 𝕳𝖔𝖌'𝖘 𝕱𝖆𝖙𝖊

'Good day to you, Mrs Brown.'
      With reluctance, I placed down the hat I had been fingering, lifted my petticoats from my shoes and the market muck and tiptoed across the street, close enough that I might converse politely, but not so close that I should be obligated to stay beyond what I wished to.

The elbows of the well-rounded woman seemed to span from one end of the market stall to the other behind her exquisite display of bread, buns, cakes, and pastries, heavenly treats to delight any gentlewoman's eye. The warm, sweet smell of them brought water to my mouth as I imagined biting into one.

'I understand I am to congratulate you, Mrs Brown. It is the talk of the town that your cakes at Mrs Hayward's laying-in were an outstanding success.' Cakes and pastries were always a safe topic of conversation with Mrs Brown, since she rightly considered herself an expert on them and could be relied upon to talk endlessly on their splendidness.

'I am indebted to you for your kindness, Abigale. It must be admitted that many compliments were laid upon me for the honey cake, but it was my recipe for banbury cake most often begged of me thereafter. Why, when Mrs Gape the Mayor's wife stopped by to congratulate Mrs Hayward on the birth of her son, she declared before every person there how she desired to be as clever as myself in making such pleasing recipes.'

Mrs Brown's husband ran the baker shop near our home and had no need for a stall when the shop did so well for itself but, for Mrs Brown, it was the means to other ends. If the reason was not merely for the feathering of her own cake-making reputation, perhaps it was rather to further her social standing in other ways.

Over many years, I had gained a strong belief that she ran her table for the sake of fishing for hearsay, morsels with which she would bait larger hooks in order to capture upstanding men and women of St. Albans. Indeed, I had seen instances of her using such wiles when calling upon good neighbours as well as town aldermen. Even if they were able or impolite enough to close the door on her, they would never be fast enough to escape her hard-gathered lures and would quickly find themselves obliged to listen out of reluctant curiosity. I was certain she called me over to discover if I had any such tidbits.

'Indeed, I remember how delicious they are.'

I searched for something more to say before bidding farewell. I need not have stretched myself. Mrs Brown had enough to say for the both of us. She readied herself to speak of other things. Her face lost its greeting and her mouth made a spout from which came words that barely moved the rest of her lips.

'Abigale. Might I call you by name?' Without awaiting an answer she went on. 'I consider myself a good judge of character, and I am certain you must agree, for Mrs Gape herself has said so often enough.' She placed her hands down on two of the bread rolls on the table so they disappeared beneath her flesh. She was accustomed to eat more of her husband's bread than was good for her, and I never once saw her refuse a sticky bun or sweet cake in all my years of knowing her. I suspected I might find myself in the same predicament if I was tempted every day with such toothsome sugar cake, countess cake, gingerbread, macaroons, apple pies etcetera. The sweet smells sung to my nostrils even paces away. She continued, 'It has come to my notice that some of this parish are in need of guidance, and I wonder if I might beg your assistance?'

I turned to see if the girls stayed by the bonnets. Indeed they did. They held their hands over their mouths, barely concealing that they giggled and twittered over my predicament. I could not have been more tempted to call them over, but showed mercy and spared them a conversation with our neighbour.

'What is it that concerns you, Mrs Brown?'

'You know me, Abigale. I do not make it my concern unless it is of the highest importance I should do so. I am not some busy-body that cannot keep my nose free of the activities of other persons.' I could think of nothing inoffensive I could answer to that, so I merely nodded. 'Then you must also know my fears are quite justified.'

Again she stopped, perhaps to allow me to placate her. The most I could manage was a 'Do go on, Mrs Brown.' There was no stopping her at any rate.

'The problem we have, Abigale, is to do with one you are intimate with, which is why it is fitting I should come to you about it.' My curiosity was ignited despite myself. 'I wonder if you cannot guess to whom I refer.'

'If I had no notion before, Mrs Brown, I am sure I do not know now. Perhaps if you did not spin the tale so long and came to the point of it?'

My neighbour frowned, took up the two rolls she had in her hands and added them to a pile that much resembled that strange Egyptian structure, the pyramid. I did not think it possible I could trouble her feelings, but it seemed I may have done so. I was about to beg her pardon when she spoke again.

'You and I are worldly women, Mrs Harris, and it is for that reason I assure myself you will know what should be done.'

'Of course, Mrs Brown. You are bound by good reason in your concerns.' I wondered if I might affect a rescue from my girls, but they now talked between themselves. I resigned myself to hear Mrs Brown to the end.

'As I said, it is for the reason of your knowing the one I talk of I come to you. I am of the mind that this cannot be tolerated.' She seemed to expect an answer of me. Having none, I was forced to ask her outright.

'What cannot, Mrs Brown? To what do you refer?'

'Why, you cannot think it reasonable! I am of a mind to take this issue to my dear friend, the mayor. No,' she answered herself, 'that will not do! No less than the midwife licensing committee will serve. We cannot have such goings on. If one man is let into the laying-in chamber, where will it all end?'

The blood prickled as it left my cheeks, causing me to seek the salts of hartshorn from my soft leather purse. I pulled the stopper and waved the small glass bottle beneath my nose, bracing myself for the effects, which came quickly. The needles of vapour burned my nostrils and eyes, so I pulled my head back, blinked and gasped deeply. Straightaway, the faint went away. The sounds, smells and sights of the market flooded me in their clarity; my heart drummed a new beat and the blood heated my cheeks once more.

I could not have Mrs Brown raising her voice about this to all the market so, allowing my better judgement step down hard upon reluctance, I came closer to the baker's stall. With my eyes cleared, I could not help but notice and be enticed by the glints of the sun on the sugar crystals. And now the smell of ammonia had gone from my nostrils the sweet aromas of cinnamon and almond rose sweeter and spicier than before. My mouth watered again, so I kept open my money-bag when I replaced the bottle, in case I should be tempted to treat myself and my daughters for our picnic.

'Are you overwhelmed, Mrs Harris? I expect it is the thought of such terrible violation of the rules of childbirth that has you in such a faint. Indeed, I was quite overtaken by a similar affliction when this intrusion came to my ears. Are you yet recovered?'

Apprehensive of the nature this conversation had taken, I was tempted to feign myself unrecoverable, take my girls and escape this woman's busy-body interference. If our secret was revealed, I would not have it unveiled in this way. It seemed to me, my nose awakened with the salts, that the unpleasant odour of this woman's muck-raking might better mingle with the noisome smells of slaughtered animal entrails and their waste in the meat shambles than with her husband's delicious bread. Fortunately, I did not betray myself before she continued.

'What are we to do, Mrs Harris? You must join with me against such things as this happening again!'

I paused in my thinking. I must have mistaken her meaning. She could not after all refer to that which I had originally thought.

I had believed us quite undone, that she included me as conspirator in the business she railed against. But rather than taking me to task for it, she seemed to consider me in collusion with her. In confusion, I resolved to speak no further before discovering more of her purpose.

'Perhaps it would be helpful if we made sure we speak as one before we address this to any authority, Mabel?' I immediately regretted the use of her first name, for then she lowered her voice as if we two were verily in it together.

'But of course we do, Abigale! To what other can we possibly refer but Mr James entering his wife's laying-in chamber? If he is not chastised for that, it is likely any man will think he can walk in where it is improper for him to do so, and where he is most unwelcome! It was your friend, Mrs Wright that allowed this travesty, so I ask that you will talk with her about being more zealous in this regard in future times.'

With her true concern aired, I found I was free to breath again and had no more need for the salts. I only hoped I hid my relief well enough that she would not comment upon it.

'You can rely on me to do so, Mrs Brown, although I believe the circumstances of it was nothing that could be helped. I recall Mr James so overcome by joy of fatherhood when he heard his baby cry that he quite forgot himself.'

'But you must ensure it does not happen again, Mrs Harris. We cannot allow a man to think himself allowed to do as he pleases for the want of restraint. He must be fined and castigated as a lesson to himself and others.'

It seemed in her repetition she would battle this point for as long as I would hear her on it. I conveniently remembered my declaration this morning to spend the day with my daughters, that we should amble through the market on the way to the woods for a picnic. I found myself determined that Mrs Brown should have no more of my time.

'You will pardon my rudeness, Mrs Brown. It is unlikely this will be a regular occurrence, and I am promised to my daughters for the day.'

With that, I excused myself, adding 'God be with you' only when I had half a street-width between us.

'You seem to have forgotten the cake, Mother,' said Elin as I returned to my daughters. 'We were convinced you would purchase some sweet thing for our picnic.'

All three giggled until I said, 'Alas, Elin, I fear I forgot to do so. Here, now. Take these coins and fetch us some.'

I was not surprised when neither Elin nor Mary took the money. It was Judith that earned our admiration when she set her shoulders and braved Mrs Brown to purchase sugar cakes for all of us.

At that moment came many shouts from the livestock end of the market. We stopped our chatting and looked towards the meat shambles to see ladies young and old step quickly back from the middle of the road, clearing a path for something to come through, perhaps a runaway cart or a thief. But it was neither. Through the aisle ran a large sow chased by a crowd of young farmers waving sticks.

We, too, stepped out of the way, giving the hog free reign to go wheresoever it pleased, and it was pleased to set its trotters over the wares of every shop and stall in the street. I do not think it missed one of them.

There it went knocking the legs of Mrs Brown's table, Judith running to the other side. There went the chandler's candles, the flower-seller's posies and the basket-weaver's wares. Once the hog had passed, I looked at the wide eyes of Mary and Elin, and could not but help but laugh at their raised brows and open mouths. At my guffaw, they too could not stop themselves from laughing.

Along the street, the farmers tried and failed to throw a rope over the hog's head, instead tramping the very same goods the escaped animal had toppled mere moments before. If it had not been for the loss of the stall-holders' livelihoods, we might have enjoyed it more, though, in truth, it could not have given us greater delight when first one farmer-boy and then another found himself on his backside in the mud and straw.

Judith, her lashes wet with tears, ran over jubilantly holding the bag of cakes in the air. She could barely speak for laughing.

'See how Lady Fortune has smiled upon us today. Any later and our cakes would be there on the ground with all the others!'

'Better. We are provided such diversion we could never have made for ourselves.' Mary took Judith's free hand in hers as she stepped up on the milliner's boards next to us.

Mrs Brown, that had been wailing and lamenting, saw us watching. I quickly turned to hide wicked and unbridled humour and suggested we go before she and others called on us to right the mess. In that we were unanimous and without meeting the eyes of the stall-holders, we set forth to follow the trail of ruination. We were followed by others of the same mind, curious to know the outcome of man against hog.

Before us, from the row of numerous centuries-old timber and plaster inns and taverns lining the street, for which St. Albans was long famous, hurried all kinds of people to see what all the fuss was about. Women carrying jugs of ale chased after men spilling hops from their tankards as they stumbled unsteadily from the doorways and were nearly trampled by our curious crowd. Some stood back and enjoyed the merry scene, while others joined our happy throng, but when we came across a group of monks from the Abbey, we left an arm-length around them so as not to disturb them in their holy piety.

When the road forked towards the Cathedral, the squealing hog took the narrow French Street to the right. The farmers finally saw their chance and sped down the wider Market Place on the left, splashing and slipping in the mud. The rest of the town laughed to see such a ludicrous sight, yet followed in their sucking footsteps looking equally ridiculous. How unseemly we raced after the farmer-boys to see the end of it, but a better time had perhaps not been had in the seven hundred years of the market, nor even since the Romans came here to build the ancient town of Verulamium.

The hog having gone down the other road, those persons that came from the shops and houses puzzled at so many muddied people running in the street. So, many of us enjoyed shouting to them.

'Close your door, close your door, a porker is on the loose!'

'Be quick and see the fun!'

'The pig runs the farmers for their money!'

Of course, few can resist the enjoyment of such clamour and confusion and the street filled with a crowd of both those that lived in St. Albans and those visitors that stayed here to sell their goods or who stopped on their way to London or the north. Not all were dressed for the muck-filled street and some wore their best travelling clothes, but they nevertheless stepped out into it in order not to miss such a treat. No time then to think how they or their servants might later regret such impulse when they must clean the slurry of waste, straw, hay and discarded food that seeped over their ankles into the tops of their shoes.

Mary, Elin, Judith and myself were carried along by the excitement. Judith and Elin found some friends and skipped along besides them, while Mary, sensing my slower pace, kindly reduced her step to keep me company. And it was fortunate she did so, catching me when the elbow of a man pushed my arm and I so very nearly joined others in the mud.

We were almost at Eleanor's Cross, the monument the first King Edward had built four hundred years past to mark the stopping place of his beloved wife's body on her way to London for burial. I suppose it had once been proud, but now the top was destroyed, and it stood as a sad reminder of the big war that Mary had earlier spoken of.

By the time we reached the cross, the farmer-boys had circled around the shop at the foot of the tall flint-covered clock tower, which marked the end of the two streets' divide. Just then, the squealing hog, white-eyed and trailing large amounts of straw from its back, came rushing from the neighbouring street, right into the arms of the boys. Each tried to prove themselves a man by catching it. Rather, it took the wiles of four together to outwit the frightened creature, and only then when they realised how the whole town laughed at them.

Finally and with great triumph, they roped the prize animal around the neck, took their elaborate bows and beat it soundly back to the pens to be sold or slaughtered. The crowd dispersed and we took our good cheer with us to our picnic in the woods and had a splendid day of it.

That night, perhaps after so much excitement of the day or perhaps for reason of the moon's strong light, my girls did not settle after we came in. There was much chatter between them and, despite my rebukes, they tickled each other and pulled the blankets one way then the other until even Mary complained. Twice did I have to tell Elin and Judith to quieten themselves, and twice more did I grumble that their bed was too close to my own.

While I lay looking at the four squares the moonlight made of our window, reflected by some shiny thing onto the ceiling above my bed, I dwelled on my conversation with Mrs Brown. She may speak louder and more often on her thoughts, but she was not the only one to think the way she did. I would have to shore up my guilty fear so it did not in the future show so easily.

At last, weary of their high spirits, especially since I must go early in the morning and check on Mrs Lane's daughter, I scolded the younger two that they would not let me have silence. It was only then that they settled and I was able to fall into a deep slumber. If I had known what the next day would bring, instead of insisting on their obedience I might have savoured their happiness.

3

Suspicion

Some time before daybreak, I climbed with leaden limbs from beneath the blankets and clothed myself. The floor tried to put a chill into my feet, so I was glad for the wool hose that had worked their way around my ankles in the night. I pulled them to my knees and felt in the dark for the threads I kept on the bedside table to hold them there and fastened them tight. Then I folded the tops of the hose over so they would not slip.

I had stood too long. I shivered and rubbed my arms.

It was cold enough to wear two petticoats so, over the top of my shift, I put on the first, tied a bum-roll around my waist then put on a second. Already, the warmth of the night had escaped my legs, but enough stayed in me to warm the cold under-layers. Last, I fumbled with the hooks of the matching bodice, then pulled the front down over my belly.

All of this I did with much practice and without seeing any of it. I had made it my custom to sleep in underclothes that I might dress quickly if called for in the night. I was also used to set everything out the night before, so I need not fumble in the dark were that to happen.

Nevertheless, if I could have found the inclination to go all the way over to the kitchen to light the bedside candle I might have done so but, then, the very tending of it would have only slowed my progress to the door. Besides, my night eyes were still good enough to make out familiar edges of furniture in the room. And though, without a candle, I could not see where the girls lay still beneath their blankets, the frugal light of the morning sky lent me enough light to see the shape of the bed they slept in and their gurgling breaths and occasional snorts made clear where they lay.

Not liking to go out without checking them, I did as I had done since they were babies. I leaned over to touch each of them. From the softness and shape of their hair and night caps, I could tell, as was often their way, Elin and Mary close-wrapped their arms around young Judith in the middle. Remembering the very agreeable time we had passed together the day before, my heart warmed with affection for each of them.

I did not intend to stay longer at the Lane house than to be sure Mrs Lane's girl was comfortable and wanted for nothing. Perhaps it would have served me better to stay there overnight than to come home, but with Mrs Lane's daughters visiting in anticipation for the laying-in, and her youngest sons in the other bed, I would have been obliged to either share a bed with her children or sit the night in the bedside chair.

Having tried that uncomfortable piece of furniture in the past and found it ill-suited to sleep, I made up my mind that I valued my own bed much better. However, had I known of the foolishness of my girls in the night, I might have chosen that discomfort.

But, no. Still would I rather take to my own bed when so often denied that luxury, for a baby does not care if it is light or dark and comes as often by candle-light as between dawn and dusk.

The oddest thing might then be how so many infants are drawn forth by the light of a full moon. My friend, Mrs Wright, says it is because the moon is closer and pulls stronger than the sun, but I wonder if it is rather Mother Nature's way of marking the beginning and end of the month of laying-in to her satisfaction. Whatever the reason, with the moon so bright this night, I held the notion the Lane girl's delivery might not be long in the coming.

My foot kicked the medicine bag I forgot I had set by the bed and the bottles clinked together. There was no use in silencing them. As I crossed the room to find my boots lined up with the others by the door, they chattered together like feeding birds. I expected the girls to wake, but neither did they stir when I put that noisy bag down to lace my shoes nor when I picked it up after. Even so, once I had thrown on my scarf and red cloak, I went out into the early morning with as much care as I could muster.

It took much skill to rock the bolt up and down that it might scrape slowly across in jerks but, alas, despite my care it came loose all at once and jumped loudly to clang against the metal holding-ring. With a measure of conscience, I looked behind me into the darkness. I could see nothing, so I listened.

It would have been fine justice had I woken the girls, but it would have served no purpose. So, finding them unmoving in the stillness, I placed my finger in exactly the right place between the top of the latch bar and the staple to prevent the two bits of iron clunking against each other. In that I also failed, but the girls had their night-ears and the noise did nothing to wake them.

A cold wind rushed past me as I pulled open the door and pushed myself into the shadow of morning light. Even before the wind caught the door and slammed it shut, the welcome smell of new-baked bread from Mr Brown's bakery enticed me forward. Sometimes it seemed Mr Brown never did sleep, for he had already lit the lanthorn outside his shop ready for early customers. Even if I came betimes, before any other man or woman opened their eyes, he and I would pass that early morning time exchanging observations about life, only ending when Gabriel rang to call the town to Angelus and the apprentices to a new day.

This morning, as usual, Mr Brown let me in so we could share the morning news as we were wont to do. As it happened, there was no news of any great note to discuss, so we talked of the farrier newly arrived at the blacksmith's and how he seemed of decent character.

'I have heard he is come from London with a son but without a wife.'

'And what is that to do with me?' I asked, understanding Mr Brown full well.

Mr Brown, a man a mere five years my senior, had in my opinion but two faults.

His greatest fault was Mrs Mabel Brown, his wife. He adored her with all his heart though he could have had his pickings from any number of suitable women. Blinded by marital affection, he believed the happiness he had with Mrs Brown to be something extraordinary, she apparently being a 'charmingly congenial woman' of 'inestimable delightful wit and intelligence'. If I had equally often thought otherwise, I did not say so. In my experience, the nature of his wife was entirely opposite to everything he believed it to be.

Apart from this serious blindness with regard to his wife, his own disposition was not without integrity and honesty, and his reputation for fair weighing of the loaves beyond dispute. He was in ruddy health and his almost plain face was very nearly always friendly after six o'clock in the morning. Almost plain, I say, for his insistence on keeping his crow's nest of an unruly red beard upon his chin gave him the appearance of a scoundrel pirate which, being in the middle of Hertfordshire, stood absurdly out of place.

Of more curiosity than fault was that his wearing it long seemed to defy intelligent nature, its presence quite contradicting the twofold reason he gave for never wearing a periwig whilst baking. Often did I argue with him against the foolishness of keeping it so long. If he had apologised once, he had apologised a hundred times for not wearing his periwig, but nerry once did he admit fault in his unfathomable beard.

In the case of the periwig, he was more conscientious. Oftentimes did he beg pardon that the heat of the oven made it too unbearable to wear one and at other times claimed that it could not be at all clever to risk long hair by an open fire. To prove him right in this, much of his beard was singed into tight fragile curls at the ends or scorched right off. As for his head, it was only unfortunate that he had lost so much hair at such a young age and had been quite bald for nigh on the thirty years I knew him.

His second fault, and fault it most certainly was, made him insensible to my discomfort when he told me I was in need of a good husband.

'Is it not time you found yourself a man to marry and help you with your girls?'

'I do not need assistance, Mr Brown. If ever I had need of any, it was twenty-one years ago when I took on young Mary. Finding a nursemaid to care for her when I was so green a midwife and had little enough work was a testing time. But I am done with rearing the girls now and, if I must take on any more, for it seems it is in my nature to do so, the girls will help me with it as Mary has done with the younger ones. I make no complaint now, for they each pay for their living and I am content with the way of things.'

'No need to chop off my head for only noticing what's what, Abigale. It seemed to me that the farrier is in need of a wife and you are in need of a husband.'

'Indeed, no, Mr Brown. You are very much mistaken. And I will have you keep such things you notice to yourself and not say them to other persons. Talk is rife enough without your adding to it!'

'I beg your pardon, I am sure. My opinion is for you, Abigale, and no other, of that you can be certain. And though you are not of the mind, perhaps it would not be too unwelcome for you to think on it awhile and see if I am not right.'

His sadness in offending me was sincere and I could not but feel regret for my sharp tongue.

'Accept my apology, Mr Brown. I am out of sorts this morning, for I have had little sleep. The girls chitter-chattered all night, or so it did seem!'

Mr Brown put down the batch of bread he had just withdrawn from the oven and scratched the remaining tuft of hair above his left ear as if it bothered him it was alone. Then he returned his attention to taking the buns and placing them on the cooling tray.

'Talking of your girls, Abigale - Mrs Harris - I must bring to your attention another thing you will have great interest in,' he said, using my last name so that I should place myself in a more formal manner of thinking

'Oh?' I said. 'And what might that be?'

'Before I tell you, I must remind you I am partial to my head and do not wish to be parted from it.' I nodded to encourage him continue. 'I see Mary and Elin being close as sisters should be, but I should warn you there is some talk of them being in the way of more than sisterly, if you understand my meaning.'

I gingerly took a hot bun from his cooling tray, as much to give myself time to compose myself before next I spoke than because I was hungry. Deep in my pocket I found a penny and placed it on the side. It was enough for this bun and three more for the girls to fetch later. Then I pinched off a small piece of the crust and enjoyed watching the steam rise from the middle, breathing deeply of the hot sweet cinnamon. I blew on it.

'I do not, Mr Brown. What do you imply? They are sisters in every way but blood. How else should they be with one another?' I placed the bread in my mouth and chewed. It was not a small pleasure to break fresh bread so early in the morning. Many a time the warm comfort of it carried me through a hard day.

Mr Brown again scratched his head, bringing blood to the skin's surface.

'I am not so bold I know how to go on, Abigale. You and I are known to each other since we came of age and we have been friends for many of those years. That is so, is it not?' I nodded. 'And you know that I am not shy of giving you a piece of my mind if it seems right to do so. Is that not also so?'

I nodded again and placed another piece of bread in my mouth. I chewed slowly, keeping my mind on it so I did not act on whatever Mr Brown seemed to take so long to lead me to.

'Well, then,' he said, 'you must understand I am a tolerant sort of fellow and not one to lean toward making a quick judgement on the lives of persons I have no right to judge. That being said, I hear what others less tolerant than myself say as they stand and talk in the shop, and am of the belief that some things that are talked of should go no further.'

Again, he looked for my understanding of what he was trying to say. I nodded that he should go on with his point to reach the target.

'Our town is not so large, Abigale,' he said, using my first name once again. 'I have said nothing of this before now, you understand, for I am, as I say, of a tolerant nature and it is not my place to be a busy-body and poke my nose where it is not wanted, but I must speak now on this matter, before it becomes a larger issue.'

I was still thinking of what he had said some moments ago. Yesterday, I had bristled when his wife had said almost precisely the same words. Perhaps they had talked to each other on it. But where her intentions were unclear, Mr Brown's held truth that blew on the embers of growing disquiet. I found I was not so tolerant as Mr Brown in hearing the opinions of others. Nor was I so patient.

'Go on, Mr Brown. I am listening.'

'You are well liked, Abigale,' he said, 'and have earned the respect of most persons of this town, but I have heard some call you by the name of Mother Midnight.'

My smile stretched thin and did not gather enough strength to raise the edges of my mouth. It was not uncommon to give a midwife that dark name when she took in unwanted girls of the parish and, though the parish might have given payment for their upkeep, many assumed the midwife used those girls to make her home a bawdy-house and that she sold the girls' flesh to lusty men by night. But if others did such, I did not. I was no Mother Midnight. My girls were as my own daughters.

'You tell me nothing I do not already know, my friend. That is oftentimes a name erroneously paired with my trade. I am listening, but I do not have all day. I have a client to attend. Do you have more to say to me than this?' It seemed I must be direct if he should no longer dodge what he wished to say, for he would skirt it all day if he was not brought to it. Wariness made my words sharper than I meant them to be.

'I do. I will reveal to you my suspicions of the secret you have kept for all these years. I am not blind, Abigale. I have watched Mary next door as a child and then when she passed through the turbulent years to become full-grown. In my privileged position I have seen things that others will not have seen, heard thing others will not have heard.'

As he spoke, he took a bowl from the side and removed the cloth that covered it. Then he started with the next batch of buns: taking chunks of dough, placing them on the scales and rolling them between his hands into balls, and finally arranging each on the greased pan ready for the oven.

I was all ears. No matter how careful I had been over the years, I did wonder a time or two if anyone had seen anything when we were less discreet than we should have been. Never hearing a murmur about it, I had hoped good fortune was on our side and we had escaped notice completely. It seemed that perhaps we were not as clever as I had thought us. How much did he know?

'Well?' I said. 'Bring your point to the target, Mr Brown. I see you are reluctant to spill what you know, but if none of it is new to me, you may be certain you will not surprise me.'

'I am sure you must speak true,' he said. 'The rights and wrongs of it are not for me to judge, nor for me to be secret about. If you know what it is I talk about without me saying it, I need not then tell you. But if you ask it of me I will freely do so.' He stopped rolling the piece of dough he was holding and leaned toward me over the table. Even though there was no other person in the shop, nor yet would there be for some time, his voice was low and confiding. 'I know, Abigale.'

I only raised my brows. I would not confirm what I was not certain of, and I was not yet certain he spoke of what I hoped he did not. His next words confirmed my fear.

"When Mary was old enough to become a young woman, I saw... her.' He stopped, I presume, to save my ears from the fullness of his tale. At my continued enquiry he finished. 'I did not mean to, but there she was facing me and, before I could look away and let her be private, though she did not know she need be, she lifted her dress to unburden herself. Understand, I could not help but see her piss. If I could unsee what I did then see I would have done so.'

The revelation that unburdened him made me heavy. The new weight of my arms had me lay them down on the counter with the remains of the hot roll in one hand and a small uneaten piece in the other. I wet my lips so that I might speak.

'So. There.' I tried to appear matter of fact, though the pricks in my cheeks told me the blood had gone from them and my seat had become unbearably hard and uncomfortable. 'Was that so difficult to say, Mr Brown? I am glad you were open with me about it, but I hope you will not be so open to anyone else, for it is not a thing I would have talked about around the town.'

He was taken aback by my dismissal of his revelation, but I did not want him thinking, friend or no, that he could hold it over me, even if he had no intention of doing so. He raised himself to full height and became more grave, if that were possible.

'It is not what she is that is wrong, Abigale. God creates every person with His own hands. He knows what He does. I am reluctant to say so, but I must tell you, it is what you have done that I must question. Concealing it, that is something I cannot believe is right.'

In that he surprised me, for I had assumed his concern was with Mary. I felt myself in a court, judged harshly by him as one of my peers and did not like it. Perhaps, for that, I defended myself too strongly.

'You do not know everything of the case, Mr Brown. If you did, you would know I had choices to make, difficult choices, and I did the best I could by them at the time.'

'Did you though, I wonder? How can you be so sure it was the right one, when you have hidden what Mary is from every woman you have tended. Is it not fitting that they should know? And what of Mary and Elin? What of the goings on between them? It does not sit at all well with me, and I do not know how it can sit right with you.'

'And since when have I sought your opinion on it, I ask you!' I took to my feet, little as my legs wished to obey me, and faced Mr Brown. At this time, even if he did stand high in my affection, he seemed more threat than friend. I did not know what I should say to him.

'You asked what I know, and I tell you that I have pieced together one or two things and found that it is not altogether something I can fathom, but I know what I have seen, and that is that Mary is not at all what you will have us believe, nor will it be long before you cannot stop what is inevitable. Mary has come of an age that, well, it may be that neither you nor she can prevent her true nature from showing.'

In saying that, Mr Brown could not prevent his own gentle nature from showing. He blushed in the way of a young man courting his love, though it was not love but discomposure he displayed. His face and his beard warred with each other for the strongest colour.

'And you would know what that is, would you. Mr Brown?' Frankly, I did not like his saying such things out loud when I had so long congratulated myself on successfully keeping them silent. In one hand I carried the half-eaten bun, and with the other I picked up my bag, the bottles clinking loudly in a way I rather they didn't. 'I thank you for your kindness, but I cannot think you know anything of the matter, I tell you. If you did, you would not have known what to do about it any more than I.'

He looked both contrite and confident. He nodded in acknowledgement of what I said, but added, 'I have told you I am not a judge of it, but I must warn you that others have noticed all is not as it should be and you would do well to heed my warning.'

With that, I lifted the door-latch with the back of my hand and used my foot to pull open the door, jangling the bell as I went out into the street. Before I closed the door again, I turned back and said, 'Since you have shown yourself a good friend to me and to Mary, for which I thank you, Mr Brown, I hope I can rely on your continued discretion? We will perhaps talk upon it another time, and perhaps we will not. But if we do not, know that I am grateful for your kindness and I will take some time to contemplate what you have told me and to prepare myself for the worst.'

With that, as the sun lit a thin line on the horizon, I hurried toward Dagnall Street and Mrs Lane's daughter Sophia.

4

The Secret

'No, Mary. Say no more. You will do as I ask. It is a trade decent enough for both man and woman, the only difference being the cloth not the tools. It will suit us, suit you, very well.'

Though not gentleman-bred, by giving fair warning, Mr Brown had nevertheless behaved in the manner of one, quietly expressing his suspicions with the decency of an honourable man. In particular, it is known by all women that a man, especially one that owns a shop frequented by nearly all of the town, might be expected to prattle almost as much as any woman. Mr Brown had not, and for that I was thankful. Nevertheless, he had posed me a problem I had yet to solve.

I had tested my ideas on it as I walked to Dagnall Street, then again throughout my walk back through the empty market square toward home. So great was my distraction that it was not until I was homeward bound that I noticed the skinny young, straw-haired man standing in the pillory. For once, I had no interest in who he was or what he had done. Nor, it seemed, had he done enough that any other person was encouraged to break from their day to throw harsh words or old food at him. He wisely stayed very quiet and did not draw attention to himself. So, I too ignored him.

And in so doing, it pleased me to find in my ongoing walk a satisfactory answer to my problem. But it was not until the passing of two days that I now had opportunity to talk to Mary and she was not, as I had surmised she would not be, at all happy with my idea. Worse, she was provoked to stand against me.

Of late, apart from our picnic three days since, Mary often hung her chin upon her chest, perhaps more than ever I remembered her to do before. Perhaps more so even than the blushing days when she became a woman and had too often mumbled her words to the floor. Not so this time. In uncommon defiance, she raised that chin of hers to boldly face me.

'It will not suit, Mother! I have no wish to change my course. Rather, I would continue the path you have had the wisdom to set for me. I am quite content to work beside you.'

'Nay, girl. It is too dangerous. Already there are some who suspect we keep a secret and if we are discovered in it your fate will be sealed. With discovery will come shame and I will not have the both of us tarred by that brush. If you take a different trade it will not be so shoddy on the either of us.'

'But the living of a midwife is what I have aimed for the whole of my life! What if I insist this to be the craft in which I continue to earn a living? If you send me to a different craft and then your deception is never discovered, I would be destined for a life of sorrow and destitution of spirit without reason.'

The spring sun, that had moments before lightened everything in the room, and had caused a few stray lengths of straw on the floor before the window to shine particularly brightly, dipped behind a cloud. In its absence, the chill of the room touched me.

Mary was generally fearful of change, but I knew in this she had reason, for the life of a good midwife was for a woman more assured than most any other; providing comfort and security to any that worked hard at it. Nor could any deny the good living and reputation earned by it. And Mary was already earning such a reputation, for she was diligent and caring in manner and my clients found her personable.

Though I was not prepared to tell her such, it came down to this. I was too old to change out of the trade. At one-and-twenty, she was not.

'I know, Mary. And I am sorry that we must take this course, but if Mr Brown suspects something amiss, how long before his wife or other person with even less care, if that does not stretch the imagination too tight, might talk out loud and without restraint? Our living might be made impossible. Worse would be the pain of discovery of our deception. Even though you are innocent in it and have only obeyed me in keeping your silence, as my deputy, my ward and my daughter your name would be as black as mine. Doubly so, for you are the subject of the secret I ask you to keep. Furthermore, if I am made unacceptable to my trade for want of honesty, then you also would lose your trade. Better that we should find you a new one now, while you have the freedom to choose.'

'I do not wish to oppose you, Mother, but I do not choose another direction. In many things, you have proved yourself right. My wit is sharp enough to know that. And it is true that often you have known what is best for me. But in this you do not. My only wish is to continue beside you in the birthing chamber. I want no other employment.'

Mary came and placed her arms around my waist and held me close. I wrapped my own arms around her and we embraced for a while. Her arms had become so strong I could barely take a breath, but the exotic sweetness of lavender she had sewn into her bum-roll comforted me. While we stood there, the sun took turns to shine bright and hide its face, sometimes adding to the fire's warmth, at other times giving the need to be by it. We took our warmth from each other.

Mary's body was gentle against me, her small soft breasts resting higher than mine, almost as if she were the mother and I the child. When had she become so tall that she must bend over to lay her head upon my shoulder? Her knees touched mine where she crooked them to better come down to my level as she tried to continue as the child.

'You cannot doubt I would never in my life give away our secret, Mother. And, if I do not, then there is none other to do so. Is that not the whole truth? And, if that is so, I cannot understand your wish to rid me from your side and deny me to work with you.'

Her voice was muffled where she rested her face against my neck. Her warm breath the breath of my child full-grown. From the day I saved this child and took her in, my devotion to her was complete. None could love their own daughter more than I loved Mary: her interest in the smallest things; how deeply she loved and with such sensitivity to the sentiment of others; her sincerity and how she embraced every flower and birdsong, every tree leafing in spring, every duckling and newborn lamb with her wonder of life.

And yet, of late, unhappiness cloaked the person she was before. Apart from times such as the day of our picnic, when respite lightened her load, the joy had gone from her. I had thought she might have been affected by a man or lack of one, and that I would hear of it soon enough. But perhaps it was more than that. I held her still closer before taking her shoulders and standing her a full arm's-length away, seeking the answer in her beautiful but sad eyes.

'What ails you, Mary? I do not refer to our talk now. I see you often cloak something from me of late. You are not so good at hiding your secrets as you suppose. What is it you try to hide from me?'

I smiled to stop it being an accusation, but still Mary's eyes opened wide and she clenched her jaw.

'You are mistaken, dear Mother. I have nothing to tell you.'

Her smooth denial saddened me. It was not in her nature to lie, but she dropped her eyes, so revealing her falsehood.

'Will you not share with me? You cannot hide your having a burden, only what it is, and you know I will discover it in the passing of time.'

Mary searched my face and saw the truth in it.

'I have nothing I need tell you,' she said.

'You might be inclined to tell me when you are ready, but it would be easier if you do not wait so long the obstacles to your speaking of it become more difficult or impossible.'

'And it may be that whatever it is you imagine my problem to be will lessen with time in the way of pain and loss and love.' Mary cast her eyes down to study nothing on the floor, and would have set her chin upon her chest once again had I not taken it with my fingers and raised it such that she should look at me. Even then she did not. Her eyes found what was behind me. Whatever she hid, she was determined I should not discover it.

'You are wrong,' I said. 'Not all things lessen with time. Some things grow. As do concerns that are not addressed.' Mary shrugged her shoulders and I let go of my grip and let my hands fall to my sides. 'Do not mistake Mistress Time as your friend, Mary. It may seem that way when you are so young and think you know her so well, but you will find she only lulls you into believing she will keep you company forever. But then, the older you become, the faster she runs away from you until at last you are chasing her, trying to keep up with her. And still she does not stop. In the end, she will leave you fallen by the wayside while she continues on her way without you.' I spoke with my inner eye on my life now gone, almost forgetting the point of my words. I drew a deep breath to bring myself back to Mary's troubles before I continued. 'Spend no more days in waiting for the right time and place to ask for assistance with your concern, for that is time wasted. Mistress Time will not come to you when you need her, I tell you.'

'That is more of concern for you, Mother, than for me. Time and I are still on the closest of terms and she does not hurry away from me as yet. And what is of concern to me is not always a concern to you. There are some things you can do nothing about and some things I do not ask you to.'

So, I had the right of it. With this confirmation, I allowed myself to be gentle in quizzing her, for it did not seem she was yet ready to reveal the cause of her unhappiness and I did not wish to force her into being angry at me for such intrusion. I spoke softly.

'Have we not shared every hardship together? Let our sharing of it be the diminishing of the thing on which you dwell. Or even, perhaps, the disappearing of it.'

'If it was something that you could change, I would surely tell you, but I am grown now and there are some things you cannot do to take the hardships of life from me. I am sure you would try, but I do not wish to bring you into my concern at this time when you can only try but cannot succeed in helping me. If I am unable to master my problem, I will bring it to you in the broadness of time and listen to whatever advice you will give me. Until then, let me alone that I might dwell on it and solve it as I see fit.'

'If that is your wish. But, again I say, do not wait until it has become more than either one of us can find answer to.'

'You underestimate my ability to do so, for you still think of me as the child I was. I am a child no longer and assure you I am much improved at addressing my own dilemmas.'

Some problems we had shared and addressed over the years were more trying than most, but we always faced them together. Not only those to do with Mary and myself but, as well, those that arose when I first brought home Elin, then Judith. Mary's welcome of them and her aid when times were difficult were a blessing to me. Her early wisdom often shored me against doubt and hardship.

Indeed, I would usually believe that whatever demons now sat upon her shoulders, with good fortune her wit and strength of character would save her when I could not. But it seemed to me that those demons of late were not so easy to be rid of.

No, I could not leave it entirely alone.

'Before I am silent on it, tell me one thing, Mary, and be artless in it. Does the heart of your concern lie with our secret and your not telling of it? Tell me the truth. I can always see if you do not.'

Mary smiled then.

'It is indeed uncanny how you are always able to see through any veil I try to hide behind, Mother. But I do not believe I have tried to raise such a cover since I left my childhood behind and found more reason than ever to hide away. I am grateful you embrace your greatest burden, the burden that is me, and every difficulty that comes with that encumbrance. Always have you shown such fortitude and tolerance of me. My needs are never neglected, nor do I want for love and tenderness. You carry out your duty to me with every possible consideration of my sensibilities even, I suspect, to your never having taken a husband to your side. Never fear. If I find I am in need of you and I can find no solution for myself, then I will come to you and ask for your aide.'

If Mary spoke honestly, I saw signs in her that she did not deliver to me the whole truth. She hid her hands behind her back. She could not completely hold my eyes. It troubled me that I would have to catch her in a falsehood for her to come clean and spill all of her trouble. But not now. The set of her face confirmed her unready to confide in me and her continuing unwillingness to do so.

'If it is no business of mine, then I will stay away from it, but if, as you say, you choose to make it mine, then I will hear you and aid you if I can.'

Mary's thin-drawn smile and nod was all the gratitude I needed, so I said it was a clear day, so perfect for gathering birch-sap, and suggested she accompany me into the woods. I was pleased she found this idea to be agreeable. Not only would we pass some pleasant time together but, if I was to show patience, she might find herself more open to tell me what ailed her.

5

Barnet Wood

The warm spring sunshine drew the sweetness from the flowers, grass and budding leaves as we ambled along St Peter's Street away from the busying Market Street. We swung our empty baskets, taking care not to hit the flasks tied to our sides.

On the left, we said 'Good day' to two laughing widows sitting in one of the stone doorways of the alms-houses, plaiting and making a living while they talked. And opposite, near the well outside the flint-walled church of St Peter, the vicar's wife took time from tending the graves to nod sharply in greeting. In better spirits than her, I replied with, 'A pleasant day to you, madam' and nodded back.

Then past Hall Place, Dr Allis' fine country estate in Bowgate, some cottages and the vicarage. Horses, sheep and dogs drunk from the several sparkling ponds, beside persons filling pails of water for their own use. A gaggle of geese strolled majestically as any court parade around the edge as if they guarded against thieves. And the occasional rider might stop at the rough water-hole in the middle of the road to let their horse drink.

Sometimes, we walked in the middle of the road to avoid the rain-smoothed dung-heaps and their yellow-brown run-offs, kept by the farmers at the sides of the street for the fields. Other times, we moved to the edge when any horse or cart came by. Before we came to the place where once stood the old stone cross and gallows, we took the deep-rutted road that run beside Barnet Wood.

Without planning it, we were drawn to sing age-old songs together, the same ones sung to me by my mother and grandmother around many a frosty winter fire. As they had taught me, I had taught my three girls. For a while the lightness of singing drove away our cares. In the trees, ardent birds sung to each other a different song, proclaiming their joy in finding such pretty mates, forgetting that in the weeks ahead they would stay sitting in the nest, first upon the eggs, then upon the young, and half-starve while their broods hatched and grew.

At the edge of the wood, we found the first of the trees we had prepared a week back. Even stretching tall, I could barely reach the bowl tied beneath the precise cuts in the bark to see what birch-sap collected there.

'You have placed it so high I cannot reach it,' I laughed. 'You will have to do it.'

While Mary reached up, I untied the flasks from my waist and my thoughts returned to something she had said earlier.

'The truth of it is that I never did want for a husband. Nor was there any that would have done for me.'

As Mary untied the bowl and passed it down for me to pour into the flask, she raised her brows in surprise.

'Why do you say so? You are a handsome woman and would surely have made any man content to have you as his wife.'

'It is not for the reason of having no suitors that I did not take one. It is for the reason of wanting to devote my life to being a midwife as did my mother and grandmother.'

I lied. That was not the reason. The face of my cherished childhood friend came to mind and I dwelled upon it for a while, until Mary held out her hand for the now empty bowl.

'I see no reason you could not have taken a husband as well as followed your trade,' she said.

'It is possible I might have found a man that would have let me keep my own business, but I did not. That path was never my destiny.'

In my mind my beautiful childhood friend smiled, showing her neat row of tiny teeth and I leaned forward with a long daisy-chain and hung it around her neck, laughing at something, I know not what. Then we stood in the meadow, took each other's hands and ran toward home to find her mother, who had the closest house, where we each had a cup of birch-sap cordial, my first taste of it.

Mary made a fresh cut, re-tied the bowl and spoke.

'At the least you were blessed with having the choice not to take one.'

It was unnecessary for her to say more and I did not deny it, though perhaps I should have. She had for some long time known her own destiny did not lie down that path. She would never take a husband. Would I have made it any easier for her had I told her the rest of it? It may be so. Then again, it may have made no difference. My life and hers were not the same and I must follow my own path, beside hers and perhaps in the same direction, but with different destinations.

'And you are certain it was not for my sakes or for the sakes of my sisters you did not marry?' she said.

'I assure you most sincerely, if I had wed, neither I nor my husband would have been happy.' Then my mind jumped to my Aunt Biddy's wedding day. The day, though nervous, she had started so full of joy she had told us her heart would surely burst. The day she anticipated the forging of an unbreakable bond with the man she loved. How they had laughed and danced together at the feast afterwards. Two lovers more delighted in finding each other could not have been found anywhere in the world. Not anywhere. Their eyes were only for each other. I was old enough to remember them embracing often, and in their desire to be alone, saw them stealing away together to her husband's house. The contrast between that day and the next could not have been more marked.

Mary was speaking.

'I say you have, in your decision, deprived some poor man a lifetime with the dearest, most treasured of wives. If I had the power to give someone such great happiness and devotion, I would surely do so.'

We moved from tree to tree collecting sap as we talked, she passing down the bowls and my emptying them. Streams of clear liquid spilled down the bark wheresoever it found a cut in the tree's skin, and we had made many such cuts throughout the woods. I smiled at the full bowls. They already made a good harvest for my tonic. Despite the subject of our conversation, I could not help but enjoy the day. Her words were not a rebuke but wistfulness, so I did not reply in defence but with comfort for her.

'I can only say likewise, that if any man could have chosen you for his wife, he would have been the most fortunate man alive.'

Mary smiled. 'You are too good for saying so, but I suppose I would have driven him to distraction with my incessant prattle and rapier-sharp wit!'

'You jest, Mary, but it is not unknown for a woman to un-man her husband with her wit,' I said.

She pulled her mouth down at the corners in false sadness, but her cornflower eyes sparkled through the lashes of her near-closed lids. She could not hold in her mirth and soon she spluttered as it escaped, first through a flapping of her lips against each other then as a most ungentle guffaw. The bowl she held shook, spilling sap over her hands and, without a thought, she raised the bowl so she could lick the undersides of her fist.

As she worked to catch the drops with her tongue she tilted the bowl too much. Liquid slipped over the edge and over her face. Even as her mouth and eyes widened in surprise, I could not prevent my own laughter at how very ridiculous she appeared, her cheeks wet and drops hanging from her nose and chin.

Tears running from our eyes, we clucked and crowed like a couple of chickens chased by a fox, every now and then squawking loud when we saw each other's face. There is nothing better than a hearty laugh to clear the way for better things.

When we had done laughing, I emptied what little was left of the birch-sap into the flask so Mary could replace it.

'Oh Mother. I could never marry. Whatever would you do without me!'

On our return home, we talked of all manner of other things such as the weather, the herbs we neglected to collect and her pending apprenticeship as a seamstress.

Supposing she should agree to the change of trade, which she emphatically did not, she could not decide whether or not, if she must work with her new mistress day after day, she could refrain from telling Madam Thread-Pecker, as we secretly called her, how it seemed to her that she used her beak nose to peck the stitches. I laughed as Mary mimed how the woman so often bobbed her head down each time she threaded the needle through the fabric and up again as she pulled the thread tight. Such behaviour did not at all defy her fragile bird-like appearance, only enhanced the commonly-held opinion she might better fly free than be confined to her shop day after day.

I further concurred with Mary's opinion that the twittering nature of the gentlewoman might well be a constant distraction, but I was also inclined toward the opinion that her skills were exemplary. And if Mary must learn another trade, she might find no finer teacher in the whole of the Hertfordshire than Mistress Cowley! On that, Mary stayed quiet. She preferred not to bring us in a circle to our earlier argument. It was an opinion that drew down the curtains on our pleasantness and the veil back over Mary's thoughts.

However, I was encouraged by the mood of the afternoon to explain to Mary why she must make preparations for any event. I made up my mind to tell her about Aunt Biddy, and how Mother had taught me to be strong in myself and not be swayed by the thoughts and tattle of others. But, despite the truth of such cautions forced at length into my ears, I should also tell her of my own discovery.

Throughout my life I had learned the contrary was also true, that the beliefs and notions of the persons of the town could not be ignored. Of the greatest importance was how my livelihood depended on their goodwill, depended on their acceptance of me. It had not been different for Aunt Biddy. It would not be different then for any other. It could not be different for Mary.

But perhaps another time. Today Mary carried burden enough that she did not need me to lay more upon her shoulders. After some while of listening only to our footfall, I searched inside me for less heavy subject matter that might lift her spirits. I found such a one in her sisters.

'Elin will come home shortly,' I said. Mary never did resist to talk of her sisters, and Elin in particular.

'And I have no doubt she will wish to tell us everything about her day, even if it is not in the slightest different in detail than yesterday.'

We laughed at the truth of this. Elin was uncommonly regular in her observations. It was a point of some amusement for the family that all too often we are able to speak her mind as well as she. That she had expectation we would laugh and did laugh with us at her own follies often led me to believe that she was more accomplished at acting than she would have us suspect. Perhaps she would also have us believe her a fool that her other accomplishments might seem diminished and I would not further my decision that she would be a good fit for a nurse-maid or some such at a house of quality.

Rather, she chose to earn a pittance with the washer-woman when there was no work plaiting straw. And, even when, as now, there was plenty, I sometimes wondered if it was for sympathy with the mother of eleven she continued to go there even when she could earn more at home.

'And what of Judith?,' Mary looked toward the market as we came back into the town centre. 'Like as not, she is already home from the market and sucking straw.'

'I fear she will never leave the house unless it is to sell her work and buy more straw. She is so fast in it now that I am quite at a disadvantage and cannot make more than half that she can. So long as she has straw, she will not want for a pretty penny.'

'Without her, likely the whole hat trade of England would fall.' Mary laughed and I laughed along with her.

As we passed Catherine Lane, we came across Dung Jack, so nicknamed for his chosen trade of shovelling muck into his cart to sell to local farmers. The fields began to reek of the particularly gagging sweet smell that rose off them in the spring. I did hear say that this man, born John Leach, made another penny or two from rabbit droppings, but if that was the case, he must be a very patient man indeed. I could not imagine a task so tedious as hand-picking the small dung-berries from such a small creature. They were of such a pathetic nature when one compares them to what comes from a horse, hog or cow.

John raised his tattered hat and gave a small bow as if we were ladies of leisure which, I supposed, we must seem to such a man. I did wonder, when taking payment for his wife's delivery, how many bags of rabbit dung he would have had to pluck from the ground to pay for it.

'Good afternoon, Mr Leach. Fare you well this day?' I looked to the cart. 'If your cart is already so full, it must be a busy market today.'

I could not well see his dirty face for, although he held his hat to his chest and did not return it to his head until we moved on, he bent his head as if he were my servant. All I could see was his brown hair hat-flattened to his scalp.

'Aye, Mother Harris. I cannot complain. I took a good cart full earlier and you see here another.'

Being so close to his pickings, I did not wish to stand long enough to do more than agree with him. I had no more to say to him, nor him to me.

'Well, Good day then, Mr Leach.'

'That man is much cleverer than any give him credit,' said Mary looking back. When I raised my brow in question, she explained, 'He will never want for a day's work. He makes his living from the dung of both man and animal. And if it were not enough that he make his living once-over, his living comes two-fold. Once from the mayor for clearing the market and the other from selling what he has piled in his cart to the farmer for the enriching of his fields!'

'I had not thought of that.' And without thinking of it now, I moved faster as we neared home, for I was in need of some refreshment after carrying the heavy flasks in the sun. Forgetting my plan to stop Mary working with me, I spoke without thinking. 'Will you visit Mrs Lane's girl? I saw her this morning and she is close to her time, but I will bottle this birch sap today if she is not yet in need of me.'

'If you wish it, Mother.'

We parted ways before we reached home, I with the promise of having ready a large cup of ale for when she returned. That she did not appear morose as earlier was a blessing for which I was thankful.

But it was a blessing that did not last.

6

Call to Duty

While Mary cooked at the stove, and Elin and Judith split and sucked the straw they plaited into strings for the nearby hat market, I set about preparing my large bottles for birch sap. Even before I had found them all out from the cupboards, Mary arrived back with the news the Lane girl had gone into town for ribbon, so one must presume she did well enough without me.

As predicted, Elin told of the health of the washer-woman and her children, her concern being for one of the youngest, suffering from some ailment that had her confined to bed. Even as she called on our own concern, she countered this with a merry tale of another of the brood slipping on a wet stocking and falling into the washtub. We were each of us content to listen to her chatter until she turned to her younger sister. 'I suppose you had assistance in carrying the straw home, Judith?'

Each time we had fresh plait-straw, the pile of it was so great it filled the corner of the room we kept for it. It seemed to bring light to that dark place. It also seemed our home grew larger when dark corners of it were useful.

'Aye.' Judith watched her hands cross each other over and again from right to left and left to right, every now and then running fresh straws through her lips to wet and soften them.

Of us all, she was the quickest and made the tightest strings. Her great skill and deftness of hand had earned her good reputation with the plait-buyers so they always gave her plenty of work and often saved the best straw for her. It could not be argued against that, as long as she could buy fresh straw or it was given to her to fulfil an order, she could better maintain herself in this trade than if she took another or she went into service. That is why she spent all of her days and evenings sitting quietly amidst a pile of straw, either by the warmth of the fire or, like the laughing widows before, on the doorstep in the sunshine, depending on the season.

Not so Elin, for though she was able to make a shilling now and again, her fingers were neither nimble nor quick. Nor was it in her nature to sit so still and in the same occupation for hour upon hour of the day. But of an evening it was different. We all four of us often sat around the hearth, keeping company and nattering whilst we made the plaits, mended a stocking or perhaps sewed together the pieces of a new shift.

'Well?' I said. 'Who did you have assist you?'

'It was the boy that carried the straw to market. I did not ask his name, only that he bring me back what little was left in his cart. It was the end of the sheaf, though still of the finest wheat-straw.'

'That must be the blacksmith's boy,' said Elin. 'I recall him at the barn dance two months since.'

'Oh! Of course. I thought I had seen him before.' Judith seemed to remember.

'How could you remember him when you were not there? Do you not also recall, you stayed home with a cough? It was after you took sick with the cold.'

'If it was not that place it was another, for I do remember him.' Judith sulked that her memory was found to be at fault.

I listened to their usual prattle while I wrapped the tall handle of the boiled kettle with a cloth and removed it from the fire I had lit for the purpose. The extra warmth did not overly bother us on this chill spring evening. Besides, I had need of a shawl once I had cooled from the warmth of the day. With two hands I lifted the kettle and poured the water into the bottles resting in the wide pan on the hearth. I had long since discovered it to be the best way to remove old potions before filling with any new liquid, as well as the preventing of green mould.

'I must commend him for his care in stacking the straw close and not leaving such a mess as did the last boy. You must have him come back next time.'

'Yes, do. He is a very pleasing boy,' said Elin.

'Yes Mother.' Judith's answer was merely a nod to my instruction.

'Supper is ready.' Mary dipped the wooden spoon into the pot, took it to her mouth and blew on it before tasting. Then she breathed through her mouth and waved her hand, for she had not shown enough patience and it had burned.

'Oh,' she huffed and puffed as she talked, no burn preventing her tongue from wagging. 'That is the boy who stole his friend's fishing stick. He took such a lashing over that.'

Mary looked pointedly at Elin, a look that was returned with raised brows. I suspected Elin had been teasing Mary. Did Mary like this boy?

'I only have the corks to do, then we shall eat,' I said.

Lifting my skirt, I sat on my heels while I placed the corks in the bottle necks so that the steam would clean them also. Then came a sharp rapping at the door with the iron horse-shoe knocker and a dulled, 'Mother Harris. Mother Harris.'

I pressed the last cork into the bottle and, placing my hand on the floor to keep from falling, pushed to my feet and went to the door.

It was young William Lane of Dagnall Street.

'What do you want, boy?'

'Mother Harris! I am sent to find you.' The red-faced boy huffed. 'You must come at once. Will you come? Ma says to tell you my sister is in dire need of your service and the baby does not sit right.'

'She was fine this afternoon,' said Mary, perhaps defending that she had not seen the girl earlier.

'Of course, boy. I will find my bag. Is your sister at home?' Already, I had pulled on my bonnet and now crossed the room to where my bag sat by the door.

'She was in the market when great suffering overtook her. Bent double, she was. Someone hailed farmer Gumbard and his wife, our neighbours that live across the way, who were at the time riding past and had them carry her back home in their cart.' He took a breath and then added, 'She made it altogether too hard to do. First, she would not stand to get in, then she would not sit or lie down.' Perhaps I did not appear to be suitably impressed, for he added, 'And she complained all the way home!'

As I picked up the leather bag in which I carried my various tools and lotions, again disregarding my earlier resolve, I told Mary to bring some of the broth in a covered pot and come with me. I did doubt we would be back by candle-light or even the morning. There was no use in looking for any other midwife to assist me when I knew Goodwife Dunwell to have gone into the country to tend a client the day before yesterday. It was unlikely she would be back in town today, for she had told me the woman in question was not yet ready for laying-in and, indeed, might not be delivered for another week or two. And my friend, Mrs Wright, visited with her daughter in London, intending to stay there for several days.

Without question, Mary did as I asked of her, for she had accompanied me to the birthing room since she was old enough to be of assistance. Despite it being spring and the air being warmer of late, as an afterthought I took down my red cloak from the peg and whipped it behind my head to sit on my shoulders. Even if it was not cold outside, I was reluctant to leave the fireside warmth and would keep as much of it as I could with me.

'Run ahead and tell your mother we are on the way, William,' I said. Then to Mary, 'It is most fortunate you are here, Mary. I believe I will have great need of you. I think you must remember the Lane girl's last baby? Recall, it was of a most awkward nature and tried as hard as it might to come out sideways. If this one is of a similar nature, we shall need the both of us to position the mother.'

When the market bustled with stall-holders, shop-keepers, farmers, pan-handlers and peddlers, one could only describe it as the meeting of town and country. All things made or created in the fields were destined to find their place eventually in St. Albans Market. And every townsperson relied on them doing so.

Since the very beginning of the world, different parts of the market place variously displayed flesh, fish, vegetables, grain, leather goods etcetera that all folk coming there would know where to sell and where to buy. If someone were to blindfold me, still would I know each area from the smell of blood, sea-salt, malt, tannins and piss.

I was often of the mind that, dragged from their green fields and warm barns, animals must know it was the end of their lives when they stood in that mucky place. Their rolling eyes and shouts for freedom did indicate as much. And, if I were to be led to the pens, the cacophony of bleats, snorts, moos and clucking, along with the smell of muck, would be enough to warn me I was by the sheep, the hogs, the cows or the chickens.

Winter or summer, one often need wear ankle boots on market days, else the dung slipped over the top and wet your stockings or hose, if such were worn. Then, every person in town was thankful for Dung Jack and others like him. What happened to the dung the rest of the year I did not know, for I only knew the roads were piled with it early spring, then the fields stunk of it before the crops were sown.

We passed the Town Hall on our left and headed toward Flesh Cross by the Fish Shambles, then right into Dagnall Street, not needing to go through the rest of the market square. Now, past the end of the day, the square still bustled with folk standing, or sitting if they could find a place to sit, tipping back tankards of ale filled at the many nearby taverns and inns. The most ideal of men had gone home to be with their wives and to do such work that needed doing before dark. But oftentimes, more so in the longer days of summer, a few made a day of it, spending some of their earnings in their cups before putting whatever remained in the family pot.

At the far end of the old and narrow street of French Row, heading toward the several inns by the Clock Tower and the Great Cross, one such man seemed to be lost in hearty revelling. Even as we turned into Dagnall Street, though I did not look to pay attention, his loud singing drew comment from Mary. 'Did you see how he so nearly fell over when old Gabriel struck?' Eight o'clock. Curfew. Time for the men in the street to finish their drinks a little smarter, before the crier came to send stragglers home, if they did not stay in town overnight. I did not envy the task of the constable to bring the reveller home, if he remembered where he stayed! None paid Mary nor myself the courtesy of tipping or raising their hat or saying, 'Good evening, Madam, Miss,' for we sped through there unconcerned about such niceties nor looking for them. It seemed sometimes our red cloaks made us quite unseen, which also had the benefit that we were rarely waylaid.

Then we were to the house of the Lanes.

Much noise, much shouting, came from within.

None answered the door on the second knock, so we went in.

7

A Midwife's Trick

'Breathe girl. You must wait 'til the midwife—' The voice of the good Mrs Lane travelled to us through the door along with much moaning.

'I am here,' I said, coming to the top of the stairs and into the bed-chamber. 'Stand aside that I might examine her.'

We walked into a darkened room, lit with candles and smelling of their burning fat as well as the baked goods that sat under the cloth on the side for us to enjoy later. It smelt strongly of sweat too, as much from the toil of working women as from the girl in labour. Over it all was the familiar birthing smell that came with the flow of released fluids, straightaway telling me how far along the girl was.

The laying-in chamber was set.

Warm smells were all bound tight to the room by the custom of closed windows, curtains and door, and mixed with acrid smoke occasionally wafting over from the fire that crackled and spat and kept evil demons at bay.

The Lane girl's mother, aunt, sisters and other gossips stepped aside to let me through. Mary followed closely on my heels. There were about six or seven women before I and Mary came, a decent enough turn-out. Those that were not busy with the birthing sat away from the bed out of the way and knitted or sewed and talked when the noise was not too loud to do so. I had been at more than one laying-in where straw was provided for women to work on plaits while they kept company, but this was not one of those laying-ins. Mrs Lane was for the old way and, in her mind, the old way was sewing and embroidery.

The girl, Sophia, lay on the child-bed with her bare feet rested against a wooden board and her legs crooked in readiness for birth. But I was relieved to see that some person had sensibly arranged pillows beneath her thighs to raise them above her body and head to prevent the baby coming too fast. If indeed the baby was troublesome how it lay, it might be necessary to raise her further yet so that I might turn it. That, then, was my first task. I must discover how it lay.

'She has been set in her travels since the market. We have tried to ease her throes, but they are too strong and come too fast.' Mrs Lane raised her voice above her daughter's groans.

I placed my bag on the floor nearby. I also found it necessary to raise my voice to be heard.

'What difficulty does she have?'

Mary stood behind me and looked over my shoulder as I lifted the girl's skirt from the side of the bed. Her underskirt was soaked. The skin was broken and the waters already released as I had known from the smell they would be.

'The baby is not head nor foot. If it is belly or arse, I cannot tell.'

With nine children of her own, Mrs Lane had plenty of experience of being delivered and less of the delivering, quite the opposite of my own understanding, but still she was competent enough to feel the baby lay wrong.

'Mary, give me some grease,' I said. Mary opened the pot, took out a large dab of duck grease, wiped it on my hand and re-sealed the pot. I rubbed my hands together. It brought to mind that I might sometime have a lady of quality to serve and should buy some oil of lilies or almonds as instructed by Mrs Sharp in her excellent book 'The complete Midwife's Companion'. This duck grease would not do for such quality. 'Mind, Mary, I need some sweet oil.'

'Some what?'

'Sweet oil,' My voice hung too loud in the air when Sophia momentarily paused in her protests.

'You want sweet oil?' Mary said. Already she had lifted my

bag and placed it on an unused seat to search for it.

'No. Only remember to remind me.'

As was oft the way, when I was ready for the examination, Sophia's mother came around to see what I did to her daughter, part to satisfy curiosity and part for reason of a mother's natural safeguarding.

'When did she last take sustenance?' I asked, again speaking louder so that I might be heard above the girl's noise. It was not only an old midwives' trick, but it was one I often found effective, talking about other things to divert attention from what one did with the hands.

'She was at the market for some hours. She might have eaten a pudding or pie there.'

'Did you eat at the market, Sophia? Have you had a pudding or pie?' I asked her.

She shook her head. Her hair was stuck to her face, wet with exertion as if she recently came in from the rain. Her lids wrung tears from her eyes, while one of her sisters I did not know the name of squeezed water from a cloth over a bowl then wiped the girl's brow.

'Mary, see if she will have a little caudle. Perhaps we can make her travels a mite easier.'

If the household had none, we kept a plentiful supply of the sweet, thick liquid, arguably the best medicine any mother can swallow. It would not take her pain when I put my hand inside, but might make it all the more bearable. As it happened, there was no need to fetch my bottle from the bag, since a large jug was laid out on the side-table next to Mrs Lane's caudle cups. I remembered the set as being given to her when she was with her first child. Mary took off the jug's cover and poured a half cup as I had taught her. There was no use in pouring a good sized cup if it was spilled before it was drunk.

Sophia's sister moved aside so Mary could hold the cup to the girl's lips. She spluttered at first, but took first one sip then another. It was best given a little at the time to prevent sickness, so Mary placed the cup on the bedside table for the sister to take up. She knew my ways enough to know she should ready herself for further instruction. The sister was perfectly capable of giving the girl more when she was ready.

'Mrs Lane, hold beneath her arms on that side. Mary, take her on this. I will try to turn the infant. Try to hold her still.' Sophia screamed then squealed when I slid my arm further in. More tears squeezed from her eyes. 'Sophia, girl, see that candle over there?' When she nodded, I went on, 'Watch that flame. Watch it close. If you see it change tell me.' Even in her throes she obeyed me. The grease allowed my hand to find its target and she screamed again. 'Watch that flame, girl. Watch that flame. I must know if it changes.' Again, her mind was removed a little from the assault on her privates. My suspicions were not at all at fault and my fingers met the softness at the top of the infant's legs. The child would not come out this day if it stayed arse-down. 'It must be turned. You girl, give your sister more caudle. Plenty of it.'

Following the clever advice of Mrs Sharp, currently the most talked of lady by midwives in the great city, I tasked some of the women to aid me in raising the Lane girl's thighs further so that the weight of the baby might pull itself back into her belly. I had to stop my meddling each time her throes came hard, the tightness of her belly making it impossible to do anything inside, and resumed once she lay her head back down for a rest.

And so began the longest hour, with the infant trying to come forth and my trying to stop it.

'More caudle, girl.' I tried to curb my irritation at the slowness of the girl's sister, who seemed not to tip the cup at all, but if temper is there to serve us, mine was not to be lessened. 'Have her drink a good wallop down. She will need it. Perhaps we could all do with a cup.'

We fell into a regular sort of arrangement whereby, on each occasion Sophia rested, her sister gave her caudle. Once I found which way the baby's head and feet lay, I also took advantage of her rests and moved the awkward body a small measure into a better position. It seemed, though, that when I had it lie another way than sideways the only way it would turn was feet down, so, I bound the feet for them to come out together. By the time we were ready to receive the baby, it was more than half way out and no longer moving. All I could do was guide it as fast as it showed itself.

And then it lay there in my hands, a boy, still and with its gaping mouth and open eyes. His mother wished to hold him, but he was weak. This was common enough and I had a remedy for such apathy. Before I tied the ligature around it, I pushed the blood back from the navel-string into his belly. Even so little extra vital blood was enough to bring life back into him and his colour slowly returned.

Then I tied the ligature in the right place, not too close to his belly that his yard would become shorter than it should be in a man and not so far he would be rendered a fool with a yard too long to be useful. I took some drops from the end of the string and placed them in the baby's mouth. He waved his hands and sucked his lips together in the way a baby does. Already were the spirits back in him.

'How fares the mother?' I asked. Not a thing had passed her lips for some time.

Mary, who would normally have readied herself to take more instruction from me was not as quick as she should have been. She only now went over to the bed to check her. She smiled.

'She has enjoyed a little too much caudle perhaps, for she sleeps soundly.'

'Now, you know better than that, Mary. Shake her awake. We are not yet done. And even when we have the after-burden, she must keep her eyes open another four hours, since she is blessed with a boy. Then she can sleep for the next month if she so chooses!'

There were laughs at that. Even if a man believed his wife to do nothing during her laying-in, still must she feed her newborn often through night and day. She might have little enough sleep unless Dame Fortune smiled upon her and her infant was disposed to sleep through the gossips' merry-making. As well as that was the need for the mother's body to recover from carrying and the birth. Sleep was her friend.

But, for now, our spirits lightened with a living child child and the mother in good health. Already we readied ourselves to celebrate.

'Come now, Sophia,' said Mrs Lane. 'You have been brave, my daughter, and you have done well. Finish what is necessary and then I will fetch the sweet treats and we will soon have you back in rude spirits. We shall all enjoy a little nibble, I think.'

Mrs Lane shook Sophia more heartily than Mary, and I questioned Mary with my brows, for she did not usually shrink from such things.

Mary looked not at me but at the baby. Neither did she respond to my enquiry nor help more with Sophia. Instead, she said to Sophia's aunt, Mrs Lane's sister, that at that time held the baby, 'Give me the baby that I might attend his needs.' Then she took him from that woman's arms and held him close for a moment, smiling when his little hand came close to her face. She kissed it playfully, then shook herself and became practical once more, looking around for where the things to wash, oil and wrap the baby were laid out.

'Indeed, you bring cheer with news of treats, Mrs Lane,' said a woman whose large chins indicated she might have attended many a laying-in merely for the pleasure of the sugar-paste. 'A feast shall revive us all!' That she did not attend the girl in the bed nor the baby confirmed my thoughts on her reason for being there.

Mrs Lane's neighbour, I knew from a previous visit, had already boiled the water and, wrapping a cloth around the handle of the kettle, carried it to the bowl where Mary had lay the baby on the clean sheet. She added some hot water into the cold already in the bowl and swirled it with her hand.

Mary lifted the sheet to check underneath then, presumably finding it missing from the pile, asked for the cloth to wash off the birth-fluids; the cloth Mrs Lane had in her hand so that she might herself wash down the baby; a task given to Sophia's mother as a mark of respect to one that had delivered of many babies. A mite flustered, Mrs Lane nevertheless gave her the cloth without question. If Mary's actions were a surprise to anyone, they hid it well. Mary washed the baby down with tenderness then, at last seeing his grandmother waiting, stepped aside to let her oil and salt him.

In turn, Mrs Lane stepped aside for Sophia's husband's mother, a handsome woman that I could not at that time remember the name of, wrap him in his swaddle-clothes and bind him with swaddle-bands. Then he was done and Mary took him across the room to the window, cradling him and rocking him as if he were hers.

All this did I notice while I waited for the after-burden to come. And, as I waited, I nursed the hope there would be no further difficulties. Then, when all was as it should be, gave thanks to God. I cleaned up the girl's privates and had some of the women help me change the bed-sheet and make Sophia comfortable.

'She is done. Let us lift her now and wrap her in the sheepskin. Mrs Lane, are you able to take the pillow from your side? We have no further need for it.'

All women there were useful and followed my instructions, and we talked of other little things while we worked. Of the quality of the skin, the need for new candles, how thirsty we were and how soon would come the light of day.

'Find out the vervain, Mary. Let Sophia have some rest at least, even if she cannot sleep.'

Mary reluctantly handed back the baby to his grandmother and from my bag took out the bottle with vervain seeped in wine and poured some in the cup she had used before. Then Mary lay the cup gently to Sophia's lips and with patience allowed her a little at the time when she was ready.

'My husband asks for the navel-string, Mrs Harris.' Mrs Lane dropped her eyes before facing me as direct as any woman standing up for her man. 'He was concerned about the crops and did consult with an astrologer. The wise one warned him, 'beware the disguised man, else our harvest will fail'. My husband fears evil even now walks silently among us.'

'Of course, Mrs Lane. I will set it aside.' Many persons would ask for the navel-string for reasons of preventing the falling disease, for good fortune, warding off witchcraft and all manner of other things, so I was used to such requests.

By and by, we stuffed the cracks around the window and door, and when all was draft-free, lit fresh candles, puffed up the fire with the bellows and readied ourselves for an intimate feast.

'Will you have refreshment, Mrs Harris?' One of the other women, likely a neighbour, offered some sweet treats for which I was glad.

'I will, and I will thank you for it.'

It was only then I remembered the broth Mary had brought with us.

'Mary, will you place some of the broth in a bowl for young Sophia? I feel sure she must be hungry. Perhaps we might have some ourselves.'

'You go right ahead, Mrs Harris. You and Mary should have something.' It was then I remembered that Sophia had been in her throes coming from the market, so in all likelihood none other of these women would have eaten either.

'Perhaps if you have some bread, we can make what little we have go further and all of us shall have some?' I said.

In this way, we passed some pleasant time together, drinking ale and talking of this and that and nothing much until I was sure Sophia was recovered from her travels and did not suffer further with throes or convulsions.

When some little time later the baby began to yell, Mary did as she so often did with the newborn infants and took him up again. She stepped around the room with him until he slept in the crook of her arm. Her affinity with infants was touching. Under other circumstances she would have made a good mother. The other women could not help but remark upon her maternal possessiveness.

'I do believe your Mary is ready to take a husband, Mrs Harris. She clucks and spreads her feathers like a broody hen!'

'Aye, perhaps it is time to introduce her to a man she can keep company with, Abigale,' said Mrs Lane, dropping formalities with the cosiness of the warm mood. The few jugs of ale already drunk also encouraged the loosening of tongues. 'I am sure we can lend you a hand in making a suitable choice.'

Sophia's husband's mother, I now remembered to be called Mrs Cooper or such, though we were not formally introduced today with Sophia's travels already upon us, became bawdy in a way she nor any of us would ever have done outside such places as those confined to women and away from men. 'What she needs is not a husband, who can only be a burden to us, and who places more restriction than freedom. What she needs is a yard betwixt her legs and a good 'thank-you-kindly-and-good-day-to-you-sir!'

The gossips slapped their knees and guffawed. So used to this ribaldry with the women after a delivery, I did not prevent my own cackle. Even Mary smiled. And so we passed the next few hours until Sophia was ready to sleep. The month was only now begun and we would call in on the Lanes many a time before it was over. Likely we would have many other such closely acquainted times together with these women.

When I was convinced all was comfortable, Mary and I took ourselves home and left her to sleep. Our payment for this night's work would be forthcoming in the summer, for the family had nought but enough for their existence at this time of year. In the summer there would be surplus of their crops and we should be grateful to have a sack of meal to make our bread as well as coins to line our pockets.

That night, it was only in those last moments before I was lost to darkness I remembered the subject Mary and I covered today and wondered if that was the reason for her pensive mood. With the memory came another from far in the past of my mother's distress over her poor sister, my Aunt. Again, I resolved to tell Mary of that time, of that tragedy. Perhaps it would help her understand why we must keep ourselves to ourselves. Not every secret is better unveiled.

8

Mary

'How goes the girl?'

Coming from Judith, ten years Sophia's junior, this raised a smile in me.

Mary, Elin and Judith were together by the stove when I came home weary of the day. Mary cut vegetables, Elin stirred the pot and Judith stoked the stove with small logs from the wood-basket.

'As well as expected,' I said, dropping my bag at the door. Despite knowing I might be called back out, I changed my shoes for slippers. We kept the floor clean and, unlike some that did not seem to care, I would not have us walking the street-muck inside. 'Her baby lives, but remains weak in spirit.'

'Will you have a cup of ale to refresh you?' Judith already took a cup from the dresser and filled it from the jug on the table.

'Aye, I will that, Judith.' I sat myself down in my rocking chair by a fire burning with welcome. I was grateful for the crackling warmth, there being a chill in the air outside. 'And then, after supper, I will have words with you, Mary.'

I rocked and sipped of the ale and took in the warmth. Before long, my eyes closed and I dozed. The next I knew, Elin shook me awake and gave me a dish of stew, which I ate still in half-sleep, staring at the dancing flames. It would be best if I took myself to bed shortly.

But first, I must have words with my eldest. I had put it off too long.

I waited til the girls had rinsed the dishes and set the rest of the stew to cool for the morrow, then invited Mary to stroll with me. Knowing I wished to speak with her, this would warn her that what I wished to say was private between the two of us. It was not often we obliged to speak outside, having few secrets within the family, but there was no place within our small house we could speak and not be overheard. It was a common courtesy to take ourselves outside rather than ask the others to leave. Besides, I found it greatly eased some difficult conversations to speak side-by-side than to a person's face.

I had thought much since I had talked with Mr Brown. There were further words that needed saying.

Wrapped in our shawls rather than our cloaks, this being a promenade of leisure and not for the purpose of midwifery, neither Mary nor I broke the silence until we strolled passed the top of Dagnall Street toward the Abbey. I had already asked after each of them at supper, so I needed another thing to say to soften the words that were to come. I thanked her kindly for cooking the evening meal, to which she simply nodded, knowing that was not the heart of the matter.

As she was wont to do, she walked with her eyes to the ground, part I believe from a wish to hide that long neck of hers, which she had become mindful of since becoming full grown, and part from enduring the shame of her secret. In particular the shame of not being a whole woman. I was not unsympathetic to her sadness over never having come into the menses as did other females of her age. Without this mark of womanhood, she would forever be denied a family of her own and must therefore remain incomplete.

With her love of children, this was a particular spite against her, especially when sometimes I saw how she became overly tied to newborn infants, as perhaps I once did. And that was perhaps another reason for the need to learn a new trade.

'I hear some talk. Does it hold truth?' Mary responded only by raising her eyes to the path ahead, but did not look my way. I did not yet wait for an answer, but continued. 'As we have talked of before, Mr Brown supposes he might be mistaken, but imagines that you and Elin might be closer than you ought be.' Mary turned her head and her eyes affected me as often they did. No person seeing the cornflowers in them would ever doubt the goddess Aphrodite as her mother. That she also was fleet of foot might mark the God Hermes as her father. 'He thinks you are to each other something unnatural.'

'It may seem so to him, and perhaps also to you, but there is nothing unnatural between us. We are sisters, not by blood but by you, the mother that took us in. If our closeness is too intimate then I am acquainted with many that must also be tarred with that same brush.'

'It is not that you are intimate with Elin as a sister. Sisterly affection is natural and desirable. I say only that you must not hold hands and embrace as if you are more than that and must not be affectionate with her in a way that you should not be. Though it pains me to say so, if you cannot tell what is one and what the other, I would have to forbid you to be so close with Elin anymore.' I knew this to be too strong, but I was weary and in less control of my words than I would have preferred to be.

We stopped walking. Mary clenched every part of her - her teeth, her hands by her sides and her body - and in that way stood over me, diminishing me.

'You cannot forbid it when I am now come of age and may choose which path I should follow in life. How often have you told me that no matter that I am only a woman, it is still my privilege to choose from those paths God lays before me? You have said that, no matter which path I take, Madame Destiny will always hold a mirror that I cannot see further, but can only see whence I have come? And by that, you mean I can never know if I have chosen right or not. By that, I also say you cannot deny me any path that God has laid open before me, Mother. What if the best way is not as a woman but a man?'

Her brown hair should have been the fiery colour of Mr Brown's beard to be a match for her too-quick temper. She had not allowed herself to be so quarrelsome since first she came to be a grown woman, more often showing great patience with the struggle of who she was. And now, twice in as many weeks did she have an argument with me. I had forgotten how angry she could be. And with anger came insolence.

I could not help but flinch. I had know the nature of her and built this life for her. I also had seen clues that the path I chose might not be everything suited to her. But I had chosen and, once chosen, the path was set.

'Perhaps so. I did hope Mr Brown mistaken, but can it be your nature confounds the path I have set you upon?' We had stopped in the middle of the market square and the usual alehouse customers spilled into the street, but none close enough to hear what we said. 'You must not, cannot, do this, Mary. That path is not any more yours to take. You might believe it is yours because your feelings seduce you to think so. But here you stand before me as a woman. Now you have come so far along it, any other path will not only be difficult but will harm you. It is a simple thing to choose the wrong path purely for reason of it seeming to be clearer, particularly when the right one seems overgrown with all manner of difficulties. My purpose as your mother is to lay clear the way before you, and that is what I have done. I hope I can trust you have not done anything you should not. Can you give me your word on it? Can you also swear on oath you will be only as sisters to each other and not... anything else?'

It was a big speech even for me, but I was pleased to think I made myself clear.

Defiance, not usually Mary's second nature, had her lifting her nose at me then.

'I will, as I always have, give you my word that I will not reveal our - your - secret, but I cannot give my word on either one nor other of the things you ask, for I will not lie to you even if it should serve me to do so.'

'Then my greatest fears have arrived and you will be the undoing of us all,' I said with such sorrow I hoped she would relent. Her jaw remained tight, as did her fists, so I pleaded with her. 'I beg you leave my daughter Elin be. You must not take her innocence from her when it is not for you to take. Swear to me you will not do anything to risk her purity!'

'I cannot,' she said. 'I cannot swear anything but my

continued secrecy. If I am, as you say, a woman, what do you think I will do? My nature takes me in a direction concealed from me all my life by expectation and dictation and now it is revealing itself to me. I cannot be certain of defying my nature, it being what I am, the very essence of me.'

'Nay, Mary. You are what I have reared you to be, a beautiful, if wilful, young woman. You must not betray what you are to become something entirely different. I will have your word on it. Must I also speak to Elin on this? Must I warn her against you?'

'You must not,' she said. 'You will mortify her. As you say, she is innocent in all this.'

'That is the greatest truth of all and I am relieved to hear you agree. She will not be brought into it unless I see no other way.' I was pleased to see less certainty in her. She cared deeply for her sister and would not wish any harm upon her. 'You are aware, she is my charge as much as are you and, if you do not desist in whatever is causing people to talk, I will be obliged to warn her against you. She is young and does not fully understand the consequences of what you do.' I did not wish to make any threat against Mary, and paused before I felt I must. 'If I believe you a danger to Elin, you must know I would be obliged to cast you out.'

I took her hand to hold it as we walked, but she pulled it free and placed it under her arm away from me. I knew not what I expected, but I did not expect that she would, as she did, continue to walk with me toward the Abbey. I steered a path away from any other person standing or sitting and drinking ale outside the inns and taverns. Mary hung her head once more, but I saw she listened, so I pushed my point home.

'Tell me plain and without guile, Mary, and do not hide anything from me, for I will know the truth of it as I always do, have you taken Elin to bed? And do not tell me you sleep in the same bed every night. You well know my meaning.'

Mary's face might be bowed but the bloom in her cheeks could not be hid. She did not answer. I could not stop the anger rising up in me.

'What? Fool! What have you done, you insensible girl? Have

you shown yourself to her?'

Even angry for her indiscretion, still I had hope I misunderstood her body's answer and did not expect an admitting of it.

'I have.' Her words hid close to her mouth so I was not certain what I heard, but I knew her meaning from the closed way she stood.

'Odds Teeth!' My nails dug into my palms as I tried not to let others around us know of our fight. With blood hurrying to my own face I cursed her from between my closed teeth. 'Curses upon you, you half-witted nincompoop! You... you... bosom-serpent! Did I not take you in and home you though your own mother did not want you? Did I not feed you and love you? Did I not teach you to be cautious about yourself? I cannot think how you have come to be so ill-advised!'

'It was not meant.' When I grasped that she was speaking I silenced my rush of harsh words, and then tried to hear her over the ceaseless angry voice in my mind. Perhaps there was still chance that I was wrong and I overestimated the damage to us. I forced myself to listen. 'You must not lay blame upon Elin. She did not mean to touch me where she should not. Her discovery of me was unplanned by either of us.' I grabbed Mary's arm and dragged her to the side of the road as an open cart approached. None could hear us there. Mary talked as if there had not been an interruption of her explanation. 'She was surprised and... handled me. She did not know what she did and I could not help myself.'

'You can always help yourself if you have the mind to!' In my head, I could not help but imagine what she said. It was not hard to see how it might have been difficult, but not impossible, to stop herself when she had no experience of it. Then again, my own knowledge was only from the talk of others, so perhaps I was wrong in this. 'Besides the wrongness of it, do you not understand that now there is another person who might through accident or otherwise reveal what we have worked so hard to conceal all these years?'

'I had no mind, I tell you. I was overtaken by a thing more

powerful than I. You are wrong to call me a half-wit, for I had no wits at all! I was at the mercy of… I do not know what it was, for it came upon me and took my will. There was not a bit of my normal good sense left to stop me…'

This was a thing I had not considered.

Weary as I was, in my desperation, I clasped hold of any rope thrown to save me, save her. Could Mary have been possessed by the Devil? Was believing her possessed preferable to believing she defied me willingly and broke my trust completely and without care? In one instant, I was both relieved that Mary did not betray us but, and perhaps worse, I was afeared that she might have been taken by Lucifer, and that was so dire I could not comprehend it. But, if it was so, it was no wonder she could not stop herself, for it would take more than an innocent standing alone to defy him!

The last was a more compelling argument. It was a thing I could do a thing about.

'You say it was the Devil that took you? If that is so, we must discover if he still sits in your belly!'

'I did not say as much, but if in all your wisdom you say it was the Devil that took me, I believe it must be so. And if it was not the Devil, then it must surely have been witchcraft, for I had no command over myself. You know I would not, in the whole of my life, otherwise have done the slightest thing against you, against us!'

'This is far worse than I feared! You must come at once to the church and be blessed by the parson! His holy water will expel any dark fiend that hides still within you!' I became single-minded that this was indeed worse, even whilst a large part of me was pleased to have a reason other than her disregard for our safety to act upon.

At first, silence. Then, 'If that is your wish, I will do as you ask, but I do not detect anything amiss in me now, only then.'

'He is crafty, that one. If you did not know he was there before, how would you know him there now? Come, Mary. If that sly demon hides within you, we must rid you of him as fast as it is possible to do, before he takes hold and makes you again do something you do not wish. If he took you once, he might do so again. We cannot risk that.'

'I am sure the risk has passed. There is nothing amiss with me now.' Mary's jaw bulged where she pressed her teeth together.

'You may have come of age, but you must understand that Elin is a minor and my charge. I will not give you leave to seduce her again. It is unnatural and I will not allow it. And if you cannot prevent yourself, then I cannot take any oath you swear to me.'

With not a little pride and forgetting only a short while past that she did say they had done nothing, Mary raised her eyes and again defied me. 'It is too late for that, for though she first seduced me, I have seduced her any number of times since then, and she has seduced me also.'

'What? You bait me! This cannot be. Then it is too late, the Devil has already taken you and must be charged with the blame. But still, by listening to him, you bring shame upon us all. The damage may be beyond repair. Woe shall come upon you, child. I ask you again, what say you? Have you compromised my other daughter?'

If I expected a different answer, I was to be disappointed. And if I expected the Devil to fight back I was not. It spoke through her and, when it did, I did not know if I could reign myself back.

'Did I choose this path? No, I did not!' It seemed that it was Mary talking, but I knew better. 'But when it came upon us, we could not deny our feelings for each other. If I have placed Elin in harm's way, I will not wait for any other but will kill myself. When we lay together? We were filled with love and all finer feelings. It was not shame we felt then. And neither should I suffer it now!'

Despite her denial, I suspected it was shame and shame alone that had her bend her head in company and now hold it high in defiance.

'I do not know if it is right that you have such feelings, for the like of you is not common. But I do know that you are not your true self when you disregard decency and take your sister to bed, of the same blood or not. It is the Almighty's wish, of that I am certain, that you should not do so, for it says the like in His good book. Of a thing I am a deal more certain is that shame is a thing for those that knowingly do wrong.' I imparted as much feeling as I could in the 'knowingly'. 'Furthermore, it would be no more right for you to have done so as a man than to do so as a woman. You have never shown yourself to be this way inconsiderate. I can only conclude, it must be the Devil inside you that chooses to so wickedly destroy her life and yours.'

'We have done nought wrong, I tell you. Yes, we lay as we have done every night of our lives, and our affection comes from love for each other that has turned in a way more than sisterly, but no consequence can come of it since you insist we two are females together. And so, it can be of no interest to any but ourselves.'

She turned and took a few paces in the direction of home then seemed to be of a different mind. I followed her with the intention of taking her arm when we reached the church and hasten her inside to have done what must be done to rid her of the wickedness still in her. And if she would not come willingly, I would find a person to help me.

But how fast had she grasped the notion that she was possessed! As her mother, I, of all the world, best knew how quick on her feet she was. And I had given her reason she might not need to be shameful: that if it was not her actions, then she did not need own them.

Mary turned again and took me aback with the anger she then spat at me, her eyes wet with emotion and marred with red spider-web lines across the whites. I had never before had reason to fear my daughter, but now I took a step away from her.

'And the thing I know most strongly is that I have never in my life done a single thing to deserve such burden,' she said. 'Yes, I am forever beholden to you for taking me in when none other would have me, not even my mother, as you have told me over and again. Yes, you have given me everything I ever needed to live. And for that, you will always have my utmost gratitude. But though you gave me so much, I neglected to find in that the slightest regard for who I am, only for what I am not. Most of all, you must know you were mistaken in your choice of my apparel. I never did suit a dress rather than breeches! Neither did I ever suit the name of Mary.'

I saw it was a time to step back a little in stubbornness and try to find the person I had always known.

'Come Mary…'

'Do not call me by that name! 'Did I not tell you only this minute that Mary was never a good fit for what I am? I might wear it with a dress, but it does not sit at all well with the deeper feelings that complete me. It does not suit what is inside this dress. Did you not one time tell me I was once given another name? What was that other name?'

Thomas. Straightaway, the name came to mind. I pondered on the wisdom of telling her, for it could only give her more pain to know it, and decided against doing so. Instead, I appealed to her as a mother.

'If you regret the judgement I made, I cannot, for I could not have kept you if you were a boy. You are the whole world to me.'

'Not only did you judge me, but you condemned me also.'

'Perhaps so,' I said. 'But it was not meant. My only purpose was to give you a chance at one or another, but not knowing which, you understand, I had to choose one over the other. I asked God for his guidance. Perhaps he had reason for steering me the way he did, but it is not ours the reason to question why.'

'Too late, you tell me this!' She pointed her finger at me. 'You have dressed me in a skirt and that cannot be undone. Indeed, I have made my life in it. I understand you cannot undo what you have done. But I can. If I cast off my disguise now, I might find some contentment in my new apparel. By what name was I called when I was an infant?'

'It was so long ago.'

'Come now, Mother. Your memory is as good now as it was then.'

'If you had a boy's name, it was mistakenly so.'

'And if you saw what I have become, you would find it was not.'

'Are you saying…'

'I am. I am a woman in this pretence you have had me live, but I assure you that is only the half of me.'

It was a long time since I had seen beneath her petticoats.

But if this was so, it was no small wonder she hung her head on her chest every day, for this was a burden greater than the keeping of a secret. It was a burden I knew more than any other and the shame was mine more than hers. What a millstone had I weighed her down with!

'I ache for you, for what you have been obliged to hide,' I said quietly.

'And I ache to be the person I know myself to be,' she said.

'But in this I must deny you. It is impossible! I forbid you to lift the veil of my, of our, secret. This last one-and-twenty years have taken the heaviest toll on my honesty and I have paid for it many times over. I will not allow you expose us both to save yourself!'

'Then you confess you did not do it for me but for you. If you loved me as your child, you would let me be everything I am.'

'You are the largest part of my heart and will keep that place until the end of the world, but I cannot allow you to unravel me. I will lose more than you think. Not only myself, but Elin and Judith, who are in need of me for some years to come. If you reveal our secret, I will lose the trust I have for a lifetime forged with my clients and I will lose my income and become a pauper. Where will the girls be then?'

'If I reveal myself, you need not concern yourself over Elin, only Judith. Elin would be my concern then.' Mary still faced me in anger. 'I think you also underestimate Judith and will find her quite capable of providing for herself.'

My face burned as if she had slapped me.

'No, I tell you. I forbid it. And I will not speak further upon it!'

Facing her as I did, I was in the direction of home, but that would not do. I did not wish to take my anger there, where the youngest two stayed ignorant of our fight. Not giving Mary opportunity to say more, for I had nothing more to say to her on the matter, I turned again toward the Abbey and strode fast in that direction. I would not - could not - allow her follow her inclination. Not ever. It did not bear thinking about.

Nor could I remove the bleakness of it from my mind. I would be exposed, shamed, penniless. Perhaps, almost certainly, through my own error, but worsened by her deeds. It was true, I would not be in the position to keep myself, let alone any other. I would be undone, and all we had built for ourselves destroyed. No. All that I had built for us destroyed. She must not do this to me, to us. She was everything as a woman, but nothing as a man.

Beneath my anger was something worse - the truth. I caught a glimpse of it and denied it. She could be all she wanted to be and take Elin from me too.

And if I lost my reputation, it was only I that should shoulder the blame.

And if I lost everything, it would only be myself that would not find a living. All others, my children, were set, for I had seen to it they each had a trade to keep them. None would have need of me any longer.

And there it was, the fear deeper than all others. I had no reason that was not self-serving to make Mary keep the secret she had kept her whole life.

But that was something she did not know. Neither did she know the whole upshot of revealing herself, what else she might reveal. She could not know.

Must I tell her about Aunt Biddy? I had delayed it too long and it may be I had no choice in it.

And, yet, it may be too late.

But she should know. She would then understand the reason I had, for her own benefit, kept her in ignorance.

Before I had gone a hundred steps, I looked back over my shoulder to see her still standing there where I left her. Even as I looked, she turned and walked back towards home, still carrying the burden I had given her as if it would press her to the ground and crush her. How I wished we could return to the day of the picnic and her laughing.

She was my heart. I had told her such. And there she was, broken.

As was my heart.

Though she did not come from my body, she was as much part of me as if she did, and my eyes grew wet and I shook as I continued to the Abbey. I would pray for her. I would pray for an answer for the both of us.

9

After the Revelation

It was the longest month since Mary and I had argued. Still we did not speak to each other, and others had commented upon it. I had stopped going in to Mr Brown's, for he was all too shrewd about our state of affairs and all the other tattle that was in the streets. It seemed every person in St. Albans knew of our fight, and many a time did I wonder how much of it was heard by ears at the window and how much passed from door to door.

If it had nothing to do with any other person, why was it that Mary was not the only one who hung her head of late? I allude to the weight of my own shame, for our argument, for my judgement of her as an infant was only part of it. How I had treated her these last weeks was the other part.

For this month past, each time Mary saw me readying myself to attend Sophia's laying-in, and even knowing I would refuse her to enter when we arrived, still would she fall in behind me and go as far as the door. Before I stepped in and closed the door on her I would see the appeal in her eyes, perhaps she thought I would weaken, and then I would be forced to deny her. And each time the disappointment lay heavy upon both her and me. Worse, I knew this must evermore be her fate. To be denied something so important can only be likened to the denial of the love of a husband or wife when the heart yearns so desperately for it.

Every day, I prayed she would not follow me, that she would go straight to her apprenticeship with madam seamstress, but she refused to make it so easy for me. Weakened by my deep sadness, I might have softened once or twice, but feared that if I did it would make it doubly hard in the long run of it. So I stood my ground.

I wondered at such times if I had it wrong, and that I only made it easier upon myself, for I could not bear to see her in that place where she should no longer be, knowing her heart would break if then denied to be there. Worse, once the decision was made, I saw that I could let go of the guilt I had carried so long for bringing her into the birthing chamber at all and so creating this conundrum.

And there was my shame. It was I that had made this situation that would destroy her. And it was I that was now saved by destroying her.

My prayers had revealed no answer to our problem. If Mary pursued her heart and became a midwife as she wanted to be then, if she were one day discovered, it would ruin me along with her. If she did not, it would ruin her. Either way, I could not see how it would not be the unravelling of me. If I had said it once, I had said it many a time, she was my child in everything but blood. Even in that I had not told her the whole of it. Nor could I much longer bear the weight of carrying that burden.

She did not speak with me of her time with the seamstress, since she did not speak with me at all. So, I do not know how she did there, but I was assured she did at least go there, for I saw on her fingers where she had stuck herself with pins. I could only hope she might grow a passion for a new craft and it would help her forget the old one. Then, maybe, she could stop her condemnation of me.

At night, I demanded the girl come into my bed rather than allow her sleep with Elin and Judith. Though I ordered it fairly, Mary did not follow the order with good grace, but made sure each night to bump around and make as much noise as she was able before taking to the bed, and then she showed me only her back once beneath the covers. Her two sisters puzzled the reason for the change, and seemed to accept my explanation that it was for womanly reasons, though I could not imagine Mary did not right this belief in Elin at least. If she did, Elin's conduct toward me did not appear blighted by it.

I did not try to mend our differences for, in every possible way, she made sure I knew I was not forgiven, whether for my once choosing the wrong life for her, for dressing her down the last time we talked, or for forbidding her exchange her dress for breeches in the time to come. I resigned to being at fault for every choice I made.

Apart from checking on Mrs Lane's daughter and the baby boy, that at first breath did not seem would last a week let alone a month, all was quiet in the way of work. This was as well, considering I did not wish to be quizzed about Mary and how we were in a disagreement with each other. Nevertheless, such was the town that already I was taken aside by first one woman then another to be asked what it was that made us so angry with each other? Busy-bodies denying any wish to be such. I suppose I must have answered to some satisfaction, but it was no satisfaction to me that our argument had lasted so long.

The black mood that lay over our home had me more gloomy than ever, and it affected not only myself and Mary. I sometimes saw Elin passing glances with Mary so that even Judith could not fail to know how we two had said harsh words to each other. With little work to take me away from such morose spirits and keep us from clawing one other like cocks with spurs, I surmised I should rather find employment further afield. However, my quandary was that, though I did not wish to stay in my own home to be slighted, neither did I wish to take employment elsewhere and allow Mary and Elin to be alone together to do what they should not. And I could not be entirely convinced either way if I should take Mary to the parson to be exorcised.

What was I to do?

My mother had often scolded me, 'Everything is according to God's purpose, and we may or may not discover the reason for it, but it is not for us to question.'

That as maybe, but still did I require an answer and praying for one had not revealed it to me.

As chance would have it, the first part of my problem was resolved soon after, when a maid by the name of Bernice hailed from a large estate some few miles north of St. Albans to find me, her mistress having recently fallen to child and wishing to retain my services. Her laying-in was not for some many months but, being sensible, she wished to make sure we would suit.

The maid stayed with us that night. With Mary sleeping in the bed with me, the girl was able to share the big bed with Elin and Judith. Before we slept, we supped together and I was pleased to see, though it must have irked her, Mary did not behave toward me with anything but respect in front of our visitor. When the meal was done, I invited Bernice to sit with me by the fire a while, giving Mary time to go to bed before me without the show she had become accustomed to making.

We discussed if, on the morrow, we should go by foot and be a day about it, or if we should await a coach or rattler to carry us there faster. I admit to using the excuse that the mud on the roads, having for the most part dried from the winter and left cartwheel ruts in most inconvenient places, would make for a rough ride. This giving me an excuse to walk at least some of the way but, more importantly, fulfill my desire to be away from foul temper for a day.

Thankfully, and for the sake of peace, Mary pretended sleep by the time we took ourselves to bed and also when we left early in the morning, although being the deepest of sleepers, it was likely she did not have need to pretend.

The next day, although gladdened and honoured by my host's invitation to stay the night, I expressed my gratitude for his kindness, but begged his wife's forgiveness for my needing to decline. I did not feel at all happy about leaving the girls on their own with things so much unresolved.

It was for this reason that I returned home late afternoon, having stopped on the roadside to eat the bread and fruit given me by my new client for my travels. As I walked, I pondered on my delight when, on arrival, the Lady, whose name I could not remember in its fullness, being of a foreign nature, perhaps Dutch, did inform me I came highly recommended by two women. They had expressed satisfaction with my credentials and abilities and were convinced I should make the most suitable choice in the whole of Hertfordshire. The whole of Hertfordshire... Such recommendations were not so plentiful that I did not take great pleasure and pride in the hearing of them.

So, it was in lighter spirits than when I had left home that I returned ready to resolve my differences with Mary. And it was with great consternation that those spirits were so quickly dashed on my arrival.

10

𝕸𝖔𝖘𝖙 𝕾𝖍𝖔𝖈𝖐𝖎𝖓𝖌

As I opened the front door, the clunking of the latch gave way to scuffling and curses from inside. The room was not lit as I had expected, but my eyes being used to the grey of the evening, I straight away saw Elin dishevelled beside the girls' bed. Mary was equally so. Judith was nowhere in the room, an unusual circumstance this late in the day.

'Odds teeth!' This and more such unchained language escaped me before I knew from whence it came.

If Elin was a sight with her undressed hair, Mary was more so. She wore neither skirt nor corset over shift, nor shoes on her feet. I could not decide which was the redder of their faces, their humiliation so blatant I found it necessary to avert my eyes from habit before I remembered, as their mother, I was used to seeing them in their undergarments. All strength left my hands and my bag dropped to the floor where I stood. I was wide-eyed as a coney waiting for the hunter's arrow to strike until I was able to overcome the astonishment of it and gather my wits together.

Sooth! I had placed only words upon Mary's revelation and had not pictured the truth of it in my mind. My wrath had no lid to prevent it boiling and burning my gut.

'Out! Out! Out! Get out, I say!' I looked only at Mary. 'In my own home?' I waved my clenched fists this way and that. 'What can have possessed you? She is your sister! Out, I say, and take your unnatural ways with you!'

Mary grimaced as if I had struck her.

'No, Mary. Do not go. Mother, do not make her go.' Elin grabbed Mary's arm and stopped her slipping her skirt over her head. No! You cannot! Mother, stop her. She has done nothing wrong. I beg of you...'

Reluctant as I was to listen to Elin's appeal, I could not close my ears to it for long and eventually succumbed to her constant pleading and crying with resignation.

'You are right, Elin. We do not wish to bring disgrace upon us all with Mary going out in that state. Mrs Brown would undoubtedly tell the whole of the town before you had taken two steps. Dress yourself this instant, Mary. You also Elin. Then prepare your ears for the severest of words that will have you wish you rather had a beating. There lie your clothes. Do not stand so coy. Cover yourselves!'

Before even they finished dressing, I could contain myself no longer.

'You make me impotent in my defence of you,' I said, not wishing to look at them. I did not want what I said to be lessened by their attention to clothes, so I stopped myself there. They were a long time getting dressed, in all likelihood because they would have to let me see their shameful faces and could not bear it. Neither would they have any liking for what they knew would be a good scolding.

Their silence left my words hanging in the air. With so little said and most everything left unsaid, I was impatient for them to stand before me so I could unrein my anger and let it upon them.

'Make haste,' I said. 'You test my patience.'

With my arms at full length, I grabbed the edge of the mantle-piece and leaned on it for support, searching deep in the fireplace for answers. I found only anger and confusion. I thought it was only at my daughters my anger lay, but the silent words that came forth were not muttered at Mary and Elin. They were to myself. I berated myself for my part in this. It was I that had been so determined to be away from here today. It was I that had knowingly left them alone together.

I unburdened my self-condemnation, only for my anger toward my daughters and the matter at hand to return.

Impatient to speak, I pushed away from the fireplace and caught my cloak on the jar of spills as I turned. The jar crashed to the hearth and shattered, throwing the thin pieces of wood all over the floor.

For a while, I breathed hard and stared at the mess.

It was a mess I, and only I, had made.

It was not the only mess I had made.

With that, my thoughts spun about. By what right did I lay blame the whole of this on Mary? Why should she shoulder it all?

I should understand better than any other. I must open my eyes and see the right in them. If persons of the past had shown a greater understanding of Aunt Biddy, her life would surely have been less tragic. Then, too, I should not wonder, would my life have been different, less secretive. How would I behave if I did not remember those dreadful times?

Then my thoughts turned about again. In my mind's eye I saw the two standing dishevelled by the bed. With that picture in my head came my mother's face telling me I must be more determined and instill in Mary the fear of making mistakes that would unpick her.

At first I paced, then I sat, then I paced again. I could find no situation where the shock of what I had seen could be put aside that I might think. And what I must address was of such serious and Devilish nature, I must find some calm before I approach it, in order that I might bring wisdom rather than prejudice to our meeting. If any of my clients came to me with a difficult question of this importance, would they not expect my wisdom to be unbiased? Why then did my daughters deserve anything less?

Then they stood before me, hanging their heads as if I would chop them off. It seemed that Mary's deportment was like a disease and Elin had already taken ill by it.

First I had to satisfy another concern.

'Where is Judith?'

Elin's whispered 'She visits with the parson's daughter' was quiet as a breeze through autumn leaves.

'What? At this hour? The bell will soon ring.'

'Yes, mother. She is to return before it sounds.'

'Well then, we do not have long.' I observed the tops of their heads. 'I am sure I do not know what to say to you,' I said at last, with every intention of saying much more.

Mary mumbled something that sounded somewhat like 'Then this day must herald as the first'. I almost answered, then saw that to do so would be to take it to something of less importance. So, I let her sore words go unmarked in order that I might take control of this runaway cart. What matters, when a loose cart runs without a driver - a few spilled vegetables rolling off the back or grabbing hold of the reins?

'Why, Mary? Why have you done this? Why do you risk everything? I cannot fathom it.'

She did not answer.

'Did you not fully understand my meaning, Mary, when we talked before? How is it you come to disobey me, so plainly and so cruelly? Do you have such little regard for me you could not wait and see how I resolved this for you?'

Even as I said the words, I knew I had come no closer to settle anything in my head. In all honesty, if honest I could be in this, I did not have any single idea of how it might be done, except for leaving behind everything I had made for myself here and moving to a different town. Or the city. Or even to the barbaric country of Scotland. Even thinking of that caused my mouth to clam shut. Nay, I could not do it, nor could I think upon the matter without a stirring of fear for what would be.

Twice Mary looked up as if she would say something, and twice fast averted her eyes. In the silence, I heard the wind blow in and out of my nostrils. The third time she raised her head, she spoke in a voice that was unlike her own. Where I expected tears, I found poise. Where I expected a rant, I found calm words. And where I expected defiance, I found contrition.

'Forgive us, Mother. We could do no other, for we are in love.'

I did not expect that. Her words took my breath, so when I

went to talk I could not. I turned my back on them while I collected myself and when I was ready I faced them again.

'In love? In love? How can this be?' I thought I was finished, but the question would not sit tight. 'In love?' I forced myself to stop the thought going about my head. 'I tell you with great feeling this cannot be. You are sisters.'

'Indeed it is true, by your kindness we were raised as sisters, but you know as well as the two of us that is not what we are. Were I the woman you raised me to be, we could only be sisters. But I am not a woman, Mother, no matter I have spent my life as one. And if I could swap out my dress for breeches as I have told you I should, then I would be a man as well as any other!'

'How can you ever be a man when you know nothing of how a man is raised?' I could not keep the scorn from my tone. It concealed something deeper that gnawed at my belly.

'I admit it as true, I am raised as a woman and must think and breathe and walk as a woman, but am I to be condemned as one merely for having been raised as one? Am I to be a prisoner in this facade, even knowing I might change my whole outlook simply by changing my clothes?'

In all my days, I was never so nonplussed. I managed only one word.

'But—'

So she continued to speak in that clear voice as a mother speaking to her child, or a master speaking to his apprentice.

'I should think I have had ample opportunity in twenty-one years to try on the garb of a woman and see how it fits, but now I have it on, am I forced into it every day for the remainder of my life without ever testing how other clothes fit? I ask you, Mother, if this is fair judgement and whether I am to be allowed to try on a long-coat and breeches, if wearing them does not pinch me and make me squirm and wriggle for being so ill-fitting? I can but ask you if that seems fair to you? If it does not, then God will guide me. But I beseech you, Mother, do what you will to assist me in changing my apparel so that I can find if I am more comfortable in petticoats or petticoat breeches. Will you do this for your child? For me?'

'I beg of you, Mother,' said Elin. Her voice wavered. 'We are not in need of a sermon from the pulpit, but of sincere understanding and… and a mother's warmth.'

Elin's impassioned plea was as sincere as that she asked of me. Having been silent so long, her outburst caught me unawares. I turned from them, with their pleas filling my ears, went to the rocker and sat. I placed my head between my hands and my elbows on my knees. I realised, despite my intention, I hadn't castigated them at all.

What should I do?

What had I done?

What sort of an old fool was I!

An old fool with no answers.

An old fool that knew no better.

Mary came and knelt before me and placed her hands on my knees. I did not know who trembled more.

'Mother, you did as you were convinced was right and I hold you no blame. I have not regretted the life you have given me, but I have found myself in need of another. I have cherished being a midwife, the joy of delivering infants into the world and if I could continue that as a man I would do so. I have loved this life with you and my sisters. I have loved most everything. But, Mother, it is as if I have only borrowed this skin. It is as if I have worn a sham skin all these years. I have the strongest feeling that now is the time to shed my disguise and reveal myself.

I could not fault her for what she said. Every bit of it made sense to me, for I had felt it to be true, even if I did not want it to be.

'Pretty words, Mary. I am convinced of your sincerity, but have you thought what kind of future you would be choosing? The life of a man is not at all like anything you are used to. If you thought that of a woman was harsh, a man's life might be a thousand times worse. You must take yourself into brutal places and be bolder than the boldest you ever have been as a woman. You may have need to fight and kill and go to war. And if not that, perhaps you would be forced to stand and fight another man with sword or duelling pistols to defend your honour or that of another.

'There are no end of differences in manner and ways, so many you cannot imagine,' I went on. 'Such things there are that you can only know if you are a man, if you were born and raised as a man. What if the breeches fit no better than what you wear now? If you are then a man, how much worse to take off your man-clothes and don a dress once again? How much worse might it be to be a man in a woman's petticoats?'

I had spoken at great length, and Mary was all too ready to take the opportunity to have her say.

'That is precisely what I am now, so it can be no worse. You do not know, cannot know. Perhaps I might take to the silken petticoat-breeches of the French. Should a man not also be allowed to wear pretty clothes? In either or any case, if it does not suit, then who am I to deny myself my old dresses?' At my face, she stopped. Then she changed her mood to make light of it. 'And who is to say I shall not be the perfect swordsman or musketeer! Perhaps my life is not as a midwife, seamstress, tailor or swordsman. I know of one place I would be welcomed as both acceptable and applauded as I am. And I believe I would be most perfect for it. I will at last join the theatre!'

Mary's wit was as always with perfect timing, when I was so ill-balanced on the cusp of change. Alongside her saucy smile, and despite every effort to do so, I could not hold back a laugh so loud I thought my bodice should split!

'Oh, Mary, I have missed you.'

'And I you.'

Mary embraced me then and Elin, uncertain and afraid of her welcome, came forward and she too was taken into our arms.

Outside, footsteps stopped at the door, then the iron of the door-latch clunked and Judith came in.

'Oh, I am overjoyed!' she said seeing us. 'I believed us doomed to spend the whole of our lives parrying sharp-edged words and fending off dagger-looks between the two of you!'

It was common for Judith to forget herself when her mind was full of the sort of things a young girl might dwell upon and enter the house without removing her shoes. It was equally common for the others of us to remind her of her forgetfulness. This was the case now. She was so encouraged to see how we had mended our broken bond that she hurried toward us, her smile big and her eyes squeezing laugh lines from the corners, but she walked only two steps before we all three shouted in unison, 'Boots!'

While we laughed together, happy to once again be of a single accord in our desire to keep our home tidy and clean, Judith leaned over, untied her boots and returned them to the door in her stockinged feet. Then, she too came over and, with the smallest arms of us all, embraced us with enthusiasm.

Though I did agree in principle to what Mary said, and she in turn did agree not to pursue any action towards her chosen target until we had discussed it further, when it came to pass, the choice was taken from beneath our noses. We could do little to stop this runaway horse after all.

11

Another Revelation

'I cannot tell you how mortified I am to be singled out in this way,' said Elin. She came clattering into the house, dropped her basket of vegetables on the floor, returned the latch to its place and leaned back against the door. She was unusually agitated. 'I offer my humblest apologies if I offend you, Mother, for you have scolded me often for talking thus, but I must tell you, that woman is the most interfering of busy bodies I have ever had the displeasure of meeting!'

'Why, Elin, you are quite out of sorts. Whatever can have disturbed you so?'

Mary hooked the needle into the bodice of the dress she was working on, placed it down and came over to Elin.

Judith said, 'If it isn't Mrs Brown, I would be quite astonished!'

Elin stared off into the distance then squeezed her mouth and squinted her eyes, mimicking what could only have been Mrs Brown in a way that was both unbecoming and witty in one, but all too accurate. "Elin Robie, you are looking in the rudest of health, if I do say so myself.' That's what she said. 'More colour than your cheeks know what to do with,' she said. Then she insulted me with such incivility and boldness it was the greatest temptation not to slap her face! Do you know what she had the audacity to say to me?' Once more, Elin squeezed her face into the lemon-face of Mrs Brown. "I consider myself a great judge of character, and if you are not with child then I am not at all a judge of it. Do you deny it?' That is what she said. And then she insulted you above all else, mother. Would you have blamed me if I had defended you?'

I cleared my throat. 'Perhaps I should know better if you told me what she did say on the subject.'

Poor Mr Brown had no inkling of his wife's true nature.

'She asked me, 'Is your mother after all called Mother Midnight?' What think you on that!' Elin's laughter came in a loud bark. 'Hah!'

Despite the severity of the accusation, both Mary and Judith laughed merrily at her, supposing her to be quite light about it. But, when she finished her act, her face squashed as if a giant hand grabbed all the edges and pulled them toward her pert nose. Hot on the tail of the laughter came a flood that might have raised Noah's ark from the ground. If it had not been for her obvious distress and the seriousness of the allegations, I might have also have laughed at her portrayal.

With a start, my eyes went straight to her belly and studied it closely. It was not possible she was with child! She could not be, for I would surely have seen signs of it. Even had she lain with Mary as the girl had told me, not a bit could come of it. For the fact is well known that two women, even when one of the two was made in Mary's form, could not create a child.

Having neither been cut cleanly from the cloth of a woman, nor entirely from the cloth of a man, though she closely resembled in design the most feminine of dresses, the Almighty Tailor had also thought to give her some masculine tucks and folds. What passed as a yard in other men was in her designed for nothing more than a betrayal of her true sex.

Elin gulped as she cried, her breath coming hard and her face flushed with belated mortification.

I should go and see our neighbour. If she had something to say and wished to cry 'whore' at me, rather she said it to my face than my daughter. Though, as I thought on it, I did remember the girl was not so lively sometimes as she had been before, but that was like as not for the general morbidity of the household of late. But, even so... did I imagine her features had become more homely, and her face more flushed than usual for so little exertion?

And was she not exhibiting such turbulent emotion that might have everything to do with bearing children? Oh my!

'I hope you did tell her she could not have misjudged it more false,' I said. Elin's eyes found Mary's and they talked silently between them. At the end of it, Mary nodded almost unseen. I would not have caught the exchange had I not faced the two of them, but I did see it and was disturbed by it. 'What do you not tell me?'

'What is it? What has come to pass?' Judith wiped her eye with her hand as if she tried to change her mood as fast as everyone else.

Mary closed the floor between herself and Elin and stood beside her to face me, their back to Judith. I cannot say this did not fill me with foreboding. I could see they were about to tell me something of the highest importance, for neither hurried to be the first to say it.

In the meantime, Judith had come around the two of them so she could see their faces.

'What goes on here?' she asked again.

'Swear you will not be angry,' said Mary to me.

'I cannot say so if I do not know what it is I should not be angry about.' She had placed me in the ridiculous position of now knowing I would likely be angry, but not knowing the reason for it.

'Say so, if you will hear what we have to say.'

'I cannot say so, I have told you. I am not the master of my feelings and they must be allowed the freedom to be as they are. They will show themselves howsoever they will. If anger should come to me, then I will feel it whether you will have it of me or not.' Mary's mouth set in a line and I knew in my heart she would not talk to me if I did not give her my word. 'I will do my utmost not to act on any anger, should I find I am filled with it and it demands expression.'

'Good enough,' she said. 'I suppose you will remember what I told you about what I have done with Elin?'

Judith's 'What have you done?' was of too little part in the larger play taking place, but enough to remind me my youngest daughter should not hear more of this. It was not for her innocent ears.

'Go outside and fetch some logs for the fire, Judith.' I thought how little time that would take her. 'Nay, take yourself to the market and get yourself some more straw to plait. You have coins enough?'

My youngest daughter did not respond. She had sense enough to know I looked for a reason to send her away but still she went no further than the back door. She dragged her feet as if a wolf lay in wait on the other side.

'Am I not of this family? If there is news to be told, I wish to hear it.'

I could not help but feel for her that she was to be excluded, but not knowing what I was to be told, I did not want her there.

'Go on, girl. Get along now. I will speak with these two alone.'

Judith retraced her steps to the kitchen and took up the wooden pail. 'If I am to go out on false pretenses, I will instead fetch water from the well. We can bear to have more and I have straw enough. That will allow you speak freely with each other.' The hurt was in her voice and I heard her unsaid words, '…that you will not share with me.'

When she had gone away, I gave the other two my attention. 'You said that you seduced her. That is of itself such a serious nature. But we have dealt with that, have we not?'

'I told you that I was possessed when I lay with her. She did not…'

That anger Mary would rather I did not have, came to me regardless that I would not have it so. It seemed she would draw on that excuse once more. 'You said so. You said you must do the bidding of the inner demon that commanded you. Have you more to say on this?'

Mary's usual defiance held good, but her shame stood in battle against it. She swallowed hard and hung her head. But the moment she dropped it she raised it, for the defiance won.

'No. You cannot make me a vessel of shame for something I can do nothing about. God made me in this mould and so He must have use for me in this design. I am not saying I am of this mind, but I am encouraged to say that, if I were a man, none would say more than 'he should sow his oats while he is young', but as a woman, I am not allowed to do so—'

'As a woman, Mary, you are wise not to do so if you do not wish to be saddled with both child and the name of 'whore'!' I bit back. 'I am sure you have more to tell me. I see Elin is not yet willing to say anything and I do not believe you have told me the worst of it.'

'You are right Mother. You are always right!' This said with more bitterness than I cared to hear. 'But, though I did say I seduced Elin it must not have been against her will as at first I thought, for she…' Mary looked at Elin's capped head, which was all she could see when the girl stared at her feet. Not seeing her face, she did not seem so sure of herself.

'She what?' I asked, knowing the answer even while strongly wishing I did not.

'She is, as Mrs Brown so shrewdly surmised, with child.'

My face prickled as the blood went from it. I felt myself sway and held my hand out in front of me in the likelihood I should fall. Though this subject was the very one on which we had been talking, and though I could see it with my own eyes, I had not given any credit to the possibility of Elin being with-child. I truly did not think it possible. For the shortest of times, I even wondered if Elin might have lain with another, but straight-away knew it could not be so.

And if Mary, even made as she was, had fathered a child, this child they said Elin carried, then I must alter everything I had thought about her, for she truly could not then be a she but a he.

Mary crossed the room to my bag and took out the smelling salts. She opened the bottle then waved it beneath my nose.

Straightaway, the blood returned to my face and my skin prickled once more, but this time with heat and sweat. I waved my hand to cool my face. Mary, seeing this, waved her hand on the other side of my face. It was not enough. She helped me to my rocking chair by the hearth and held my arm as I sat down.

'You know not what you talk about,' I said, stalling for time and praying their news held no truth, as if any delay I created could change it. 'It could not be so. You were not made that way. If it were so, there would have been more signs. It makes no sense to me, and will make less sense to any other person. Elin cannot bear your child. You must be mistaken. I cannot, will not, hear of it.'

'If you will hear it or not, it will continue to be so,' said Mary.

Elin too came to where I now sat and knelt before me. She took up my limp hands in hers and cupped them on my lap.

'I humble myself before you and beg your forgiveness, Mother. Do not only blame Mary. I am, to my eternal shame, more at fault than Mary. If I had not- Nay, I cannot undo what is done, and shall live with it for the whole of my life, but I will not regret it. It is only for the heartache it brings you I must beg forgiveness, for neither of us can undo that. As Mary and Judith are in your debt, so too shall I always be, for the taking me in when my own mother would not have me. And for that reason I am doubly mortified if I am to be the cause of your undoing.'

She stopped, perhaps hoping for my forgiveness, but I had none to give her. After our last talk, both had pledged their lives to keep the secret that would now - and it could be no other way - reveal my deception to the world. None of those who believed me honest would place their trust in me again. And, in that distrust, would lie poverty. For who would employ one such as me now? I pursed my lips to hold back loose words that might slip out before I was ready to say anything that would be useful.

'What ails her, Mary?' she asked. Then to me, 'Speak to me, Mother. What can I do that you might forgive me?' Elin squeezed my hands, lying still in my lap. I gave her back nothing. What could I give? I could give no comfort when I had none and when I was myself in need of it. She would need more than I could muster. Neither could I give hope. Any life she might have had with a husband was assuredly destroyed by her indiscretion. I could not even give my love, when it was squeezed so tight in a ball in my chest surrounded by something hard I did not recognise. I went to shake my head and found I had neither the desire nor the will of movement to make such a simple gesture.

'Leave me. Leave me be. I wish to think.' I managed at last to make a decision to be private with my own thoughts. I could not bear to look at either of them longer.

Elin took her actions from Mary, who, without a word, took Elin's top hand from where it cupped mine and pulled her to her feet. Her twenty-one years had given her enough wisdom to know when withdrawal was the wisest of all choices. The shame of it was that she had not used this same wisdom when the two had lain together.

12

Judith

The day grew darker and then even the grey dusk was gone.
I sat without candlelight. I could barely see anything but the grey edges of the cold fireplace. Perhaps I should have set the fire, not being so warm this night. It would not take much to bring a flame over from the kitchen, but I did not have so much movement in me. Behind me on the back of my seat was my evening shawl. I twisted in my seat, took it up and pulled it around my shoulders, clasping the front together. I shivered nevertheless.

None of my daughters had yet returned. Had Gabriel rung out? I could not recall. If it had, they should all have been back home. I had expected Judith to have come home quickly, for her task would not have taken long. The other two perhaps had taken themselves someplace to talk, or hide from me. But if the bell had rung it was past curfew, the tolling of which told good folk it was time to bank down the fire if they were home and take themselves from the street if they were not.

Should I have scolded Mary more? In truth, I had not scolded her at all. I had given her nothing of what was in my mind. Should I have comforted Elin? Had I felt at liberty to do so, I might have done, but my own dark feelings had warded off any such action. And now, after an hour or two of sitting, my thinking came back and I started to make plans for each of us.

If Elin did not reveal to any person who it was that had fathered the baby, suspicion would fall on every youth and man in the town until the culprit was discovered. And if none were uncovered, suspicion would flow free and easily and fingers would point in all directions. Surely none would suspect Mary, being of the fairer sex, so long as we were canny and discreet. None need ever know the true details. Perhaps, even, if we were clever about it, we might conjure up a man to have passed through the town a month or two ago, on whom we could hang the whole thing upon. Yes, that was good. If we prepared ourselves and agreed on such details as he should look like and what his trade was, then we may yet avoid discovery.

Better still might it be if the sham-father had a name. It could not harm the deception at all, for none would expect him not to have one. I thought of names. Should it be the name of a noble passing through in his coach, or an earthy farmer come to market? The first might seem as if he had ill-used Elin, playing his advantage over her to have his fun. The second would throw suspicion on every market farmer riding into town for years to come, never to settle so long as the market took place. And since St. Albans market boasted to be the best in the middle country from the beginning of time when the town went by the name of Verulamium, and would likely be so until the end of time when it would be called Armageddon, that would not do at all.

Either way, neither of these choices sat well upon me when they cast Elin into the role of a woman sorely used then instantly thrown off.

Perhaps a soldier going to war? Plenty went away to die in battle elsewhere. None would expect him to return any time soon, if ever, making the child come from a tragic affair of the heart. And it might appear that he had promised to return and marry her, that her child was a love-child even if it had worse names.

Yes, that would likely do well enough. And his name should be William, for that is a solid name belonging to an honest man and would be a good one to throw around as often as we should like. That decided, I was confident that we might pass the infant off as a love-child, even without a marriage.

Then again, if they should insist upon remaining together, which was to my mind an all too blasphemous thing, I would be forced to send the both of them to the city where none would know them. There they could weave any story they chose and none would know anything more than what they are told. Doing so would be a difficult task for me. Already I felt the loss of them in my heart. If they were to be gone from me, how lonely would I be!

Then again, it might be that we all of us were far too forward-thinking. It was early in the child-bearing. Such is the way of Mother Nature that the baby might easily be expelled for its unholy source long before we need worry about any mound showing on Elin's belly. But, was I knowing the plans of the Lord as to why Mary and Elin were caught up in this together? No, I was not. And not being given instruction how we should approach our destiny, I must do my best with the knowledge given me. I must assume that the infant would be born unless it was not. And if it was, I must lay plans for it now.

The iron latch clunked and the door opened. Quiet footsteps came into the room.

It was time I faced the guilty two and gave them the piece of my mind I had held onto before.

It was neither Mary nor Elin, but Judith, that came in the door.

'Hello? Is anyone home?'

'In here, Judith.'

'Lord! Why do you sit in the darkness, Mother? Are you ill? Are you injured?'

The thump of a full pail on the floor was unmistakable, as was the sound of spilling water.

'Nay, child. I only sit in the darkness to remove all distraction that would take me from my thoughts. I will light a candle now.'

Judith waited on the threshold while I pushed myself forward in the rocker and came to my feet. In the dark, I felt my way to the mantle-piece, where was left a candle ready to be lit, a tinderbox and a drinking cup that replaced the smashed spill-jar. The thin splints of wood moved too easily in the cup, reminding me I must buy another jar. I ignored the tinderbox, rarely putting myself to the toil of using it when I could use the kitchen fire that was nearly always burning.

In the kitchen, I lit the spill in the fire and brought a flame to the candle. I found I must guard the wavering flame from the open door with my hand.

'Come in, come in. And close the door behind you,' I said.

Judith pushed-to the door, lifted the latch and dropped it with a clunk into the iron keep, so securing it. Then she took off her cloak and hung it on the peg by the door. But she did not straight away come into the room, instead looking somewhat fearful.

'Come on in and tell me, girl, whence do you come? You were a long time fetching the water. Did you see your sisters?'

'Nay, I did not.' She answered the last first and then the second. 'If my eyes and ears did not deceive me, you did not want me here and I was out of the house as you wished me to be. I did not go straight to the well, for I would be forced to sit with the pail all this time. So, I walked through the market-place. But I must tell you, Mother, and I am certain this will be a thing that can only add further vexation to your day, but I heard talk of one of my sisters in a way you would very much dislike.'

Talk of either was nothing I would like. One as easily as the other, both Elin and Mary, might now become the fodder for good-folk to chew on. Though perhaps I may have devised a plan that would save Elin from all scorn, a veil thick enough to throw over the worst of it and conceal some of her shame. The black of Elin's name might rub off over time and she would regain her place beside all others.

The matter of Mary was of a different nature. After one-and-twenty years of keeping her name from their prattling jaws, I could only pray it would not be her reputation that was chewed on and spat out. Not that she deserved none of it, I thought, but I would rather she escape condemnation and did not, like Aunt Biddy, become the talk of every busy-body... as well as plenty that were not. If, then, she did not, as she jested, lay her hopes on the stage, then the monstrous beast of society would act to destroy her and make a freak of her.

'Of which did they speak, Elin or Mary?'

'I am sure none ever thought foul of Mary. Her affection from every mother is assured, for they value her calm manner during the laying-in and how engaging she is with their older girls and boys. She is very well talked of for such reasons. No, it is of Elin they speak. They say she has brought shame upon herself. What of this, are they wrong? Is this what you whisper about together?'

Judith's concern was apparent, the flickering candlelight shadowing the lines between her brows.

'I will be the one asking the questions, girl. Did I give you by-the-leave to speak to me so? Do I not have enough cooking on the stove without your adding to the pot? Now, tell me, who has burned your ears with such tittle-tattle as you see fit to bring me?'

'Rachael and Norman Parks, I used to sit beside in plaiting school.' Mrs Park's children? Mrs Brown had certainly been a-prattling if their mother had heard already, for they were never snug together, being equal in reputation for their tale-telling! 'Elin was not wrong in her earlier message. What I have heard can be measured on the same scale. They say you are Mother Midnight and hold a scandalous house. They say you keep young girls to sell their flesh to willing men with large purses! Furthermore, they said their mother had told them they should not speak to me since, even if I am not of her wanton-blood, I might find myself tarred by the same brush.'

'Do they indeed! And what do you say in reply to such vile accusations? I hope you are clear they hold no truth.' I barely held my tongue against such gossip, though I would gladly tell Rachael's and Norman's mother what I thought of her spreading all manner of slights about myself and my girls! I would not thank her for unravelling my own good reputation that had taken a lifetime to build. It seemed it might take a mere day to destroy.

Judith, no doubt expecting greater consequence to the drama that went before, did in her relief at my calm mood harp merrily upon our supposed crime in greater depth.

'Norman said you have two trades, the both being concerned with delivering. The one is delivering women of their babies, the other is delivering young girls to lusty men.' When she saw my face, she stepped backwards and quickly said, 'I did tell him he is right only about half of it. You are a midwife of good repute, and none can deny it, and that is your only business. And I did tell him furthermore that never in all the years I have lived in your household have I seen the slightest proof of any other trade and no men ever cross our threshold.'

'Good girl. You must keep saying so.'

'There is no reason to say otherwise.'

'That may be so, but you will be tested on that, for I have a thing to tell you that did quite astonished me and will likely baffle you. You will know it soon enough. You are right in your suspicion about Elin. It does seem there is some truth to Elin carrying and if she bears a child, then you will be questioned on it.'

'It is true then? Elin carries a child? I did not think there could be anything more nonsensical, for this is Elin we speak of, and my sister is not yet of age!' Bless the girl, she was happy and excited rather than worried. In her youth, she had no inkling about what that would mean for us.

'I have yet to examine her in spirit or body, and have not tested the truth of it, but they tell me it is so.'

Judith's face turned suddenly from joy to bewilderment.

'How can it be that Elin finds herself with-child when she has not been with a man? You have taught us often enough to know that both man and woman must come together for this to happen, so now I am certain there cannot be a wit of truth in it!

'Good girl. Tie yourself to your belief in her, for she is no whore and would never be party to letting a stranger bed her. You must say this to any that speak of it to you. Her name must not be sullied.' Then I thought of something else. 'When Mary and Elin return, we will talk further on this and the story you must hold to.'

Judith started to come into the room and, without thinking, I said, 'Boots!' When I said it alone, it was less of a game and more of a grievance. Judith obediently took off her footwear, moved to the bed and quietly took off her shawl. Still quietly, she folded it neatly and placed it on their bed. Atop the shawl she neatly placed her bonnet. Then she asked where Mary and Elin were and, not knowing, I said I would go out and find them. I was myself concerned about their whereabouts. They should have come home before now.

As a matter of fact, even though darkness lay close to the ground, I was of another mind to pair my search with the clearing of fog from my head. If I was to do battle with Mary's wits again, I would first prefer a fresh look at the facts.

'I will look in the Abbey grounds and see if they are there.' I had oft found the Abbey or fields to be the best place to think.

I pulled on and fastened my boots, took up my red cloak from the peg and departed. Donning the cloak had the usual result of joining me in the craft with every other midwife in the land, so allowing me to draw upon the strength of all that had worn it and giving me command over almost everything I would come across. And it better readied me to deal with this Pandora's box that was now opened.

Judith watched as I raised the outside latch. Before I pulled the door closed, I saw suspicion there that I did not tell her everything. I hoped she would hold her tongue, for now at least, for I did not yet know what else to tell her. Likely she would find out soon enough.

I never did reach the Abbey, nor even halfway to it.

13

Avoidance

I passed along St Peter's Street towards the market-place, hoping to see Mary and Elin, but if I did not, I would go on further to the Abbey and draw on the peace I found there.

Before I had gone so far, lit by the lantern under the sign of The King's Head, I saw Mary and Elin walk some good way before me. It was only that they took a glow from the lantern that I recognised the colours of their capes and bonnets.

As they approached the inn on the far corner of Dagnall Street, their shadows trailed behind them towards the empty pillory. Without a glance at anything but each other, they passed beneath the inn's jutting timber balcony, where stood a single gentleman leaning over the top of it to smoke one of those long clay pipes that men are joined to.

Mary and Elin did not hold hands, but their hands hung close between them. They might as well have announced to the whole of the wretched town that they did lie together! Shortly thereafter, they fell back into the darkness beyond and the waving shadows that had darted and jumped over the stones at their feet joined the larger blackness.

If I walked fast, I could catch them.

But, finding my daughters walked faster than I was able, I was forced to increase my stride. Even if I was able to run and catch them, I would not wish to draw comment upon myself from those that either still revelled in the square or were up to no good. I might appear foolish for my hurrying, but alas that did not stop me from being foolish and, true or imagined, bringing more eyes upon me.

But then, being a midwife, if it was not for my next actions, I might be mistaken for simply hurrying to a birth.

I was still too slow. Indeed, I would have to chase them for some time to catch them.

'Mary! Elin! Be still that I can talk to you!' I wheezed the words to their backs, but they did not stop. I had neither the strength of voice nor will to shout louder. I might have fallen behind if the two of them had not chosen that moment to extend their hands and clasp them together, so giving me wings upon my heels.

No. They must not! They would be seen.

I lifted the front of my petticoats and dress so as not to trip over the hem and broke into a slow trot. Slow, because it was all I could manage. My growing girth having become my biggest hindrance, I had to work to make my ageing body go faster than a slug on salt.

A woman laughed. I turned my head to see if she laughed at me. Another joined the first. Two women of mature age came from one of the shop doors, one parting and the other seeing her to the door.

I immediately knew the bare-boned one facing me was Elin's sometime mistress, the washer-woman. Perhaps it was my age, but I could never remember her name. I knew her only as the wife of the shopkeeper and that she worked herself toward an early grave to feed and clothe a dozen children, none of whom I had delivered. She was determined to have only her family at the births, they not taking any payment, and had proved fortunate in not once needing a midwife.

I nodded briskly at her and hurried on. I did not wish to talk at this time to the other woman.

The larger one, dressed in street clothes, had her back to me and was obviously leaving. It was, of course, that busy-body Mrs Brown. I should have known her broad back anywhere, even in the dark night.

As I hurried past the fleshless washerwoman, she broke off her laugh and pointed in my direction, saying something I did not hear. Mrs Brown turned and her mouth also dropped wide.

'Abigale!' It was more a shout of surprise than of her hailing me. I turned and raised my hand after I trotted past, but did not stop. I could do no more than wheeze when I tried to bid her good day.

What was I thinking! My undignified run through the street after my girls would draw more attention to them than they did to themselves. Or, rather, all eyes might be drawn to myself. I made myself slow to a more natural pace and convinced myself it was for that reason and not because I could go no further.

Now barely twenty feet from Mary and Elin, I could easily see how they smiled and talked to each other as they walked in and out of the flickering halos of lanterns, hung to welcome customers into the inns and taverns at the end of French Row. It struck me how tall Mary was beside Elin, the top of her head a full foot more than her sister's. How much taller and stronger I thought of her now than before. To my mind came a picture of her dressed in a man's fine knee-breeches and stockings, a long coat and large-brimmed hat complete with the most jaunty of ostrich feathers. I could not help the picture; it forced itself upon me. It was so real I stopped a moment to comprehend it.

All the while I observed the two of them - Mary in my mind's eye still dressed in a man's finery, Elin looking up so adoringly as she now did - I placed my hand on my chest and drew deep breaths. My old heart pained me. I dropped the front of my dress and leaned down to rest one hand on my bent knee whilst my poor beating heart tried to catch up with my legs. It took longer than I would wish and, meanwhile, my two continued on their way away from me.

'Mary!' I tried again, but came out with something resembling the cawing of a crow. Nevertheless, though it could not have been me she did hear, Mary twisted her head then, with some surprise, turned fully toward me. The moment she came roundabout, she was herself once more. Mary my daughter. Elin, attentive to Mary, wondered what it was that had turned Mary's head and looked behind her. When she saw me leaning over so indisposed, she ran to me with Mary close on her heels.

'Gracious, Mother. Whatever is wrong with you?' Elin said.

Her concern for me was comforting. My throat sore with hard breathing, I could say nothing and simply held up my hand for her to show patience. I would have her wait until I was able to speak.

'Mother, are you ill?' said Mary. 'Are you in need of a doctor? We shall fetch him.' Already she was telling Elin to stay with me, as if she needed to be told.

'Nay…' I finally croaked. 'Nay, not I. It seems I am merely too old to chase after two young persons walking at a gentle pace!'

I took some more breaths while the cool air took the heat from my cheeks. It could not take the sweat from my armpits and chest and I was aware of the sight I must convey.

'May I fetch you a drink, Mother? It seems you have run a long way.'

There was nothing at all manly about Mary now; she was all concerned daughter. I declined her kind offer of both drink and seat. Then, when I would say something more, I found I had nothing more to say and could not remember why I ran after them in the first place!

'Wither do you go?' I tried. It was as lame as old Mr Trotter's wasted leg and too weak a reason for my breathless haste. What urgency had I placed on their walking together when I had fair killed myself to prevent it! The girls, without speaking with each other, each took a side of me, linking their arms in mine, and raised me to full height, walking me slowly back the way we had come.

'Why, we only take some air to think,' said Elin. 'It seems to aid you so very well, so we thought it might be of equal benefit for our cause.'

She need say no more. I knew their cause and did not wish to speak of it in the street, where all manner of ears might catch snippets of it and pass them on to mouths that would chitter-chatter all over town. I would not repeat that mistake.

'I too came for the benefits of a fresh breeze to blow the dust from my mind,' I said. 'But it seems to have swept my thoughts clean away with the dust.'

'Shall we accompany you home?'

'No, no,' I said. 'I will find my own way.'

They argued a while on the wisdom of such stubbornness, but I convinced them I no longer needed their assistance. Indeed, if I felt any more foolish and lacking in sensible thought, I might turn my cracked-brained into the nearest asylum.

I wandered home with that sharp picture of Mary dressed as a man coming strong in and out of my head, muddying my reason for chasing the girls until very nearly when I stepped over the threshold. Then, seeing my hand on the latch and the door half-open, I brought my hand to cover my eyes.

Their hands! I did not hold against holding hands, for every young girl demonstrated affection for a dear sister or friend, but when my girls clasped their hands together it was if they embraced. If it was so clear to me now, how long before other persons might see and know? If they only suspected, they might take against both Mary and Elin. And if they did, would they close them off from society? Would they cast them out on the common shore and me right with them?

A fearful thought.

None must discover anything.

I must send Mary away.

My daughter Mary. I could not bear to live without her. Yet, I must, to save the three of us. And to save Mary from Aunt Biddy's tragic fate…

Aunt Biddy, now in my mind, took up a seat there. It was if I were back in our kitchen a few days after she was wed, and there was Mother and Aunt Biddy seated at the table with a jug of untouched ale before them. Aunt Biddy covered her face with her hands, much as I had done only a short while ago, but still the wet of her tears slid out from behind them. I cannot remember if she said a single thing, but she cried for hours and then she fell silent. Later, when Aunt Biddy had left the house, Mother was unforthcoming on the reason she was so distraught, only that her new husband had beat her on their wedding night, which was for a child more than reason enough.

Aunt Biddy was found face-down in the town pond the very next day.

It was not until I rode into womanhood that I too yearned to be endowed with a more womanly body. Mother, overhearing me, berated me for my self-flagellation of words. She warned me not to take against myself so.

'Do you recall Aunt Biddy?' At my nod she continued. 'And do you recall her here at this table not long before she died? You were young, but I suppose you might remember.' My mother, looking like a farmer's wife rather than a midwife, had her sleeves rolled to her elbows and scrubbed at the bottom of a pot while she talked. I watched her face redden with the effort. 'She came here so distraught she could not bear the burdens of the world any longer.'

When I asked her more on it, she clammed shut her mouth. Then she told me, 'You must not take after my poor, darling sister. She might have retained a life of contentment if she had never tried to marry, for she kept her secret close until her wedding day. She thought herself loved by her husband and loved him back with every beat of her heart. Yet love did not save her. Perhaps it was what condemned her.'

I asked her why, why had love condemned her? She told me then of how, on their wedding night, her husband discovered she had something of both the masculine and feminine nature. He was so incensed by her trickery, so outraged was he to be deprived of the beautiful bride he supposed her to be, that he blindly beat her to an inch of her life. It was not the beating that killed her but the breaking of her heart.

Neither was her husband silent on what he had discovered and Biddy fast became the subject of much ridicule. Even when they found her in the water, some folk did forget they had loved Biddy. 'As had her husband, they thought themselves betrayed,' Mother told me.

When I saved Mary, only her birth parents and Mother knew her true nature, and Mother warned me again, 'None must ever know. You and she must keep it secret 'til the day you die. Your lives and livelihood might depend on it.'

And so, for twenty years and more, I did everything necessary to hide any reason for ridicule or disdain from the town. It was my belief our life had otherwise been as good and wholesome as it could be.

But Mary herself might now bring the end to that. She was heedless of my warnings and the consequences of her actions risked everything for all of us.

Must I send her away to the city? It would be easier to take a disguise in London than in a small town or village nearby where too many knew the business of everybody. What if she did stay? If we kept our secret close? Would we be safe?

That was a question I could not find answer to. There had always been risk of discovery and, if we were not discovered now, there would always be in the future, but if Elin carried Mary's baby, that risk was so much greater. No matter how I thought on it, there was not a single future I could imagine where they could hide such feelings for each other.

Nay, there must be no future together. There could not be.

The thought sent me forward again. I continued into our small cottage and closed the door behind me with new purpose.

I would find some place where Mary would be employed and happy. I knew of many a midwife who might bear a good deputy, one well-trained in the art and trust-worthy. Trust-worthy in all that was important for the work, that is. Perhaps every person kept a secret and it was only time that would have it discovered. In death some secrets are found, yet other secrets carry beyond the grave. I hoped this would be of the second kind, for by then it would matter neither to her nor any other.

Though, for the sakes of her child and the mother of her child, better it should never be discovered at all. Either way, they would surely suffer if she stayed.

But… contrary-wise, would they not also suffer if she went away?

It was a dilemma for which I did not have an answer. Either way, together or apart, lay unhappiness. Nothing I saw answered to the fixing of this. Was there any path on which we could all of us be both together and happy?

As I examined possible futures, they every one of them exposed Mary and myself for what we hid from the world. And if I should devise any plan to save us from the world knowing the truth, then each of us must continue to live the lie. And in living this lie, the parts we would play would keep us from ever being wholly together.

Or whole in ourselves.

Nevertheless, rightly or wrongly, I would do what I had decided and write to several midwives of my acquaintance in the great city. Perhaps it might be better to explore instead if any knew of a seamstress that would take Mary on.

Of one thing I must be certain. Mary could not return to assisting me in my work. It would not be proper in this town where she had fathered a child. Yes, she must follow the path of seamstress I recently set her upon. Perhaps it would suit. Though she had a lifetime of being a midwife and only a few months' apprenticeship to a seamstress, she had, of course, many years of domestic sewing and an eye for good style. It would take some years to learn the finer details of the trade, so I could not count on her to earn any more bread for the table. It must suffice.

Judith sat plaiting by the light of the kitchen fire. It was not unusual to sit together around the fire, passing the time in such a way, but now she seemed uncomfortable doing so. Likely the events of the evening had unsettled her. As I came in, she ran some pieces of straw between her lips to moisten them before adding them to the plait she worked on.

As the door clunked shut, she looked up. When she saw my countenance, she immediately put down what she was doing and came to her feet.

'Mother? Are you taking a turn?'

My mind being full of other things, I did not straightaway answer her, but stared into the flickering corner of the room where the pile of straw lay.

'Judith, you must make supper tonight, a simple one. I am tasked to something important, and must do it before sleep.'

Judith obeyed without question. I was pleased not to have her argue with me. When she had finished the plait she was doing, she crossed the room to place it down with others ready for the straw hat trade. Then she returned to the kitchen fire and added a log from the hearth beside it.

Late as it was, she set about preparing the brace of coneys I had left sitting on the side, given to me in return for delivering Farmer Barnet's wife some time past.

I would not have needed to waste a candle if Judith was not in need of a place to cook, but I would be in the way of her if, as I was inclined to, I sat on the stool she so recently left empty. Instead, I took a candle to the fire, lit it with a slip and placed it in a candleholder. Then, while Judith gutted and skinned the coneys, I took myself to my favourite rocking chair. I arranged on top of a piece of wood I purposed for a writing desk my writing paper, ink pot, blotting paper and quill. Then I sat in the chair, careful to plant my feet firmly on the floor so the chair would not rock.

Only when I opened the ink pot and dipped the nib did I pause.

Until then, I had not noticed how much pain there was in my chest, and not only because of the running up and down in the street. Nor because I was old. This pain I had before, the pain of missing some dear person, that would last long after my daughter and companion of many years had gone from me. I would miss her more than she would ever know or believe, especially when she knew what I had planned for her.

14

Refusal

'I will not go! You cannot make me. I am of age.'

Mary's scowl was fierce and frightened me. Rarely did I see her so enraged, if ever. Her anger filled the room. She stood with her legs apart and her hands curled on her small waist, ready to fight me on this.

Elin was uncertain whether to hide from me or from Mary, when we had each set ourselves up with the loudest mouth and strongest voice. And so she pushed back into the wall behind Mary to become almost invisible as a ghost, but not completely so. It was not she I was concerned with at this time so I gave her no more attention.

As well, somewhere in the corner of the room, knee-deep in fresh straw and in the way she always did, Judith sat quietly by. Whether or not she continued to work on her plaits I did not know, but she made no sound. I am certain that, if she did, it was diminished by our raised voices and went unheard. The straw made its presence known more than she. The smell of it filled the warm air and its dust tickled my nose.

I could not help but give Mary a piece of my mind, for I was used to doing so, but the strength of her feeling took me aback. If I had thought she would go quietly where I would send her, I was most heartily mistaken. Certainly, though I was assured my actions were for the highest of reasons, I wavered.

That Mary did not wish to go only made me wish to follow my own desire to keep her home. But no, I had not wrong-footed my role in writing to my friends and asking them to take her in, only in the not telling them of the circumstance.

'If you will not go for my sake, then go for the sakes of Elin and the child.'

Mary approached me then, her whole body tight as a coach spring. Though she had never done so before, for a passing moment I feared she might strike me. Never before had I thought how strong were the young and how weak were the aged, but such an image of Mary raising her hand to me, though it shamed me, caused me to step back a pace. I do not remember if I held up my hands to protect myself but, if I did not, I might have.

Mary raised her brows, but her puzzlement at my action did not stop her coming forward another step. She un-clammed her teeth to speak. Strange though I think it now, it was the tears on her lashes I noticed more than her anger. Where her anger told me she would defend herself, her tears told me if she was not yet defeated, she was sorely wounded.

It was me, her own mother who had maimed her.

'You tell me what I should do? You who have designed my whole life to your satisfaction but not mine? I am not a puppet tied to a stick and made to dance as you desire me. I am not. You cannot wriggle your stick and make me fall to my knees, nor force me to follow your every direction against my wishes. I am not on the stage yet.'

Even whipped to anger, Mary's oft-used remark on her being forced to take the life of the stage had me pulling back a smile. This was not the time for humour. She had not finished.

'I follow the path God has laid for me, go where He guides me, as you have always told us we must. That is the path I must choose and no other. He has seen fit that Elin bears my child and I willingly accept and embrace both the blessing and the burden. I will not leave them to their own fate when I particularly wish their fortune to be joined to mine, nor shall I leave them to the mercy of a meddling old woman!'

'Old woman?'

Did she refer to me as 'old woman' or some other person? It could only be me. Impudent wretch! But there it was again, a cut meant to blood me in return for my own attack, not to maim me, but it cut deeper than she might have intended. Me, old. But if I had become so, when did the young stop taking instruction from their elders?

'Old woman, you call me. I should think you do as your elders tell you! If we were trees, then I am the sturdy kind that has endured many winters and borne fruit many summers. I am wise to the trials of the world in a way you cannot be. I have seen more and heard more and I am a better judge of such things than you, a mere sapling. Your tree only now begins to bud. Listen to my wisdom, the wisdom of maturity. If ever our secret is discovered, if ever the truth about you is discovered, you shall be ridiculed and cast out but, if you leave now, you may return as often as you are able and see your child whensoever you wish.'

I hoped I had struck an arrow of wisdom in Mary that might hold good. Again, she raised her brows, a fleeting recognition of the truth, but then threw my words back at me.

'If I go I may come back, but if I stay I must go? That is a twist of reason conjured by a lunatic, I am sure.'

'You dare call me lunatic now? If you cannot show me respect, how should I take your other words! With so few years behind you, you cannot understand the heads of persons as well as I. You have not seen how it is with folk. If you go, they will pair you and Elin as nothing other than sisters. If you stay, your deeper feelings will unveil themselves and betray you, a fact that Mr Brown has already revealed to me.'

Without pause for thought, Mary stopped me with a question.'

'And what of Mr Brown? If he is a good man as you have said, is it not unlikely he will make me known to the town?'

'He sees your deeper intimacy even if others as yet have not,' I said. 'And though he will not talk of it as his wife is wont to do, it cannot be long before she too makes comment upon it.' I stopped to imagine Mrs Brown as the town-crier, running from door to door and shouting about it to every person who could not close their doors fast enough. 'That one would have the whole of the town knowing our business in less than a day!'

Some of the heat went out of Mary and her shoulders fell.

'We will be considerate of that, Mother. Elin does agree with me that I should stay here with herself and the baby. I can earn as a midwife and when I have no laying-in to attend, I can earn as a seamstress or in plaiting. I will not be short of a shilling to lay upon the table.'

'You cannot be blamed for your ignorance, girl, but you are mistaken if you think you might live amongst folk who know what you are. Of one thing I am most certain, you cannot continue as a midwife now. In our business, it is a mother's trust and assumption that only women are present at the birth and laying-in, while no such privilege extends to any man. You know this as well as I. Our place in the birthing chamber is given on good faith. You have proved yourself at least in part male. It would be unseemly and against all good practice, then, to take yourself into a woman's most trusted place. But that is only a part of it. I can no longer in good conscience bring me with you.'

'There is no need for them to know. Who will tell them? You? Nay, never, for you hold the key to the secret. Who else? None but my natural mother knows what I am and she has more reason to keep our secret than reveal it. My grandmother was clear on that.'

Indeed, my mother was clear on many things. On this she was clearest. 'My sister died for how she was born,' she often said to me. 'You must stay hidden, stay secret. Never let any see. They will destroy you. They will destroy you both.'

Neither of us had moved from our fighting positions for a good time. I had all but forgotten the whole world in order to battle my point. I saw only Mary and her anger at me. Thinking of where she came from, I tried another tactic, to remind her of her roots and appeal to her gratitude of me.

'You forget your blood-father that gave you to me to dispose of. Somehow, Dame Fortune kept other womenfolk and gossips from your mother's laying-in and left me alone to bring you forth, but he is one that knows of you. It is he that I have most feared all these years would betray you, though I pray he remembers the tragic fate that befell your mother's Aunt Biddy and takes pity on you. Perhaps that is why he has, as yet, said nothing.'

Again, I was surprised at the tears in Mary's eyes. She had not cried for her natural parents since that disorderly time when a girl becomes a woman. Then she had mourned the loss of the parents that disposed of her as so much human waste, when they had wanted nothing more for her than that she be washed away with all the other stinking carcasses sunk in the animal and human waste at the common shore.

It was only good fortune that had me passing when Mr Jewett, her father, and my brother by marriage, would have tossed her in the river some months after she was born. 'We want nothing more of this one!' he had said. 'It will take from the mouths of our others when already food is little enough. It may as well die quickly now than suffer later.'

'Nay, never!' I had said. 'To do that to your daughter would be abominable. You cannot do it!'

'This be no daughter of mine and I will not raise it with mine.'

Without a single thought, I took that baby from him and told him to forget his child and that he need do no more for her! And so it was that I took home my sister's child and reared her as my own, a growing comfort for a lonely spinster. And, as I had instructed him, neither my sister's husband nor my sister took any further interest in her life. I was not certain my sister knew it was I that raised her child, for she nor I ever spoke of it, but I am certain she must have guessed.

'Have I no right to speak my own mind?' Mary asked. 'Must my sex take that from me on both accounts?'

My heart bled for her as it always did when she questioned the trials and strife laid upon her by the body with which she was born, she being the fairest of young maidens in every respect but her sex. In that, she was not treated so fairly, though I must accept the Lord God must have good reason for making it so.

'Sooth! If you were a man, you would follow your heart as you saw fit. If you were a woman, you would know your rights to be as well as mine. They would not be full, but you should know them such as they are. Many a good wife will rule the heart of a man and might gain near equal influence to her husband merely by association. You know as well as I that such well-endowed women are given leave to speak more openly about worldly things and that is always more than the wife of a working man.' I found that I had left the topic I meant to follow. 'But perhaps a person with both yard and cleft will never fully have the advantage of either. If you can accept that is so and amend your manner to being one so disadvantaged, you might find yourself more comfortable with your lot.'

Mary pursed her lips and held back anything she might have said in her defence. Not only did she refuse to accept the disadvantages of either, she contrary-wise insisted she should benefit from the advantages of both. That she could not was a woeful thing she had yet to make her peace with. I could not fault her in her dream, only her actions.

She turned from me and went to Elin, who had stood quietly by all this time, pressed against the wall. When she placed her hand on Elin's growing roundness, Elin covered it with her own, showing more than acceptance; a wish to have it there. Elin pressed her lips together and blinked eyes rimmed with unshed tears, eyes kept only for each other, eyes closed to what others saw. She never did like raised voices.

This was neither desirable nor acceptable. They could not pursue each other in this way. God Himself must be against it, even if He had allowed Elin's belly to become a fertile home for Mary's seed. Are we not told in the Bible 'Cursed is he who lies with his sister'. Was my part to prevent the fall of my children from His Grace, and should I do it with every bit of persuasion available to me? Or had He chosen this path for the two of them?

'No!' Mary broke the silence with an emphatic exclamation. 'No, I say. I deny it most strongly. I am not a lesser person because I am not moulded fully as man nor woman. To say so is odious and is to imply I am not equal to every other person and hold rights of neither one nor the other. And that is a thing I can tell you. I am as human as every other person and I have the deepest and the gentlest of sensibilities. I suffer pain when I fall or lose something dear. I am excited when happy, and maudlin when sad. And I love deeply.' She smiled at Elin but it quickly failed. 'I am perhaps an easy target for piercing arrows shot at my heart, especially when called ungainly or plain, though plain I can live with. But I am no monster to be locked in a cage of prejudice. Release me, Mother. Release me from this prison you have kept me in.'

I could not parry further with Mary while her enormous eyes pleaded with me, splitting my heart asunder. My voice trilled when next I spoke.

'My sweet Mary…' I cleared the squawking bird from my throat and tried again. 'Mary. Come to me.'

I held open my arms, and straight away she came into them. She did not bend her knees to embrace me at my height so I spoke into her neck.

'I envy your beautiful soul, my sweeting. I have wronged you and I beg your pardon if I did imply otherwise. But I am not the only person in this town. Talk is rife and even those that know me now talk of Elin and how the baby's father has left her a by-blow to keep, and they wonder how she will get by. If I am Mother Midnight, they challenge me, her fate is sealed in my hands as a whore, but if I am not, I should cast her upon the street as a wanton. Either way, her reputation will not stand here in St. Albans. Her name and that of her child are forever blackened and, either way, I too am called 'whore' or 'dark-hearted mother'.'

In our embrace and truce, I believed my words to be the end of our argument, but I was very much mistaken.

15

Mary Must Go

Mary placed her travel bag on the floor. It bulged at the bottom corners, which were worn and frayed, but the top sagged inwards. She carried few personal possessions. She had little more, but what she had filled the trunk by the door. Her coach to London would leave within the hour. Even relieved at her obedience, I was puzzled by it. I had thought she would try harder to stay.

When the turmoil overtook her and she embraced me I came close to tears.

All morning, she, Elin and Judith had sat on the edge of the bed holding each other as if it were the last time. At various times, one or other of them would look to me to see if I had changed my mind or if perhaps they could change it for me. Their eyes had in turn pleaded with me and murdered me. At no time did they acknowledge the pain in me with a softening of spirits, nor did they offer me a single word of comfort. Yet I could not expect solace when my action was so abhorrent to them. To myself also. But there was nothing else to be done.

I prayed that, despite our cruel parting, we would find comfort in the future because of it.

Mary did not cry, but in her sadness she tightened her arms around my waist and her breath came fast and loud, quivering despite that she tried to force it to be still. She rested her chin on my head and her warm breath moved my hair, and tickled my scalp. I squeezed tighter when her breaths quivered as she sucked them into her lungs. Over her shoulder, Elin and Judith were round eyed as they watched us. Mary swallowed then and when she tried to talk, she rasped like a rusty door hinge.

If I had thought her obedient, I soon found I was much mistaken. I thought us done with the fight over this, but even now, at the threshold of the door and ready to go, she proved herself unwilling to bow to my command after all. She returned again to her battle to stay. The difference this time being that she was on the threshold of leaving and I was prepared to lose my daughter to the city, perhaps forever if she chose not to return to me. I could not harden my heart any more when the sorrow of losing her sat already as stone in my chest.

'I beg of you one last time, mother. Please reconsider. Can you not imagine how we four might stand as four strong pillars to support a strong roof over the little one? Surely, we would not so easily be destroyed. Do you not see? With one of us gone the house is weakened and the roof that keeps us safe will collapse? We must stay together.'

The sense in what she said was the sense of a young person who knew nothing of the strength of an army that could lay flat a castle or hold siege around it. She still did not understand the strength of so many mouths joined together in spirit to stand in judgement against us.

I struggled to be strong against her plea. I argued again how, contrary to her belief, as long as she stayed here in St. Albans, the risk must be greater that we should be discovered in our deception. If we stood together, we would be damned together. She was but an innocent lamb in a flock of sheep. Rather than being safer in a flock, when the wolf came it would still seek out the lamb and no ewe or ram could defend it. We would be unable to defend her. She would be all so much dinner in the mob-wolf's belly.

And then we must indeed consider the fullness of belly of one dear to us…

'What is the use of revisiting this quarrel, Mary? We are done with it. Now Elin can no longer conceal her belly and people stop and ask, 'Who is the father?' it is even more urgent for you to follow our plan and leave.'

'That does not signify, Mother. What can it matter what they think? They will doubtless imagine what they wish and our answers will hold no importance. And if that is so, why should we give an answer at all? I say we should not!'

Mary, at once riled again, let go of me and stood back. I tried to remember when last she had shown that joy for life she used to have and could only think of that day we took a picnic and had such fun in the market chasing the hog. Since that long while ago, the only happiness she showed was when she was together with Elin. Trying to convince myself of a reason Mary could stay, I asked myself over and again, if I could not deny the love between them, who was I then to deny them what little happiness they might find together?

But no, it was sinful. Neither I nor the people of the town could condone it, and I could not bear to hear them condemn her. Nevertheless, she should not slight those of our acquaintance without regard for their sensibilities.

'That is no answer, Mary. The good people of this town are our friends and neighbours and we cannot have a livelihood without them. Who will employ us if they cannot place their trust in us? And how can they trust us if they see we keep secrets from them? Elin might yet command sympathy if it is believed the father of her child took himself off to war to die, for so many women suffer such desertion. If they find you are the... father of the child,' and it was with some great difficulty I made myself say those words, 'not only will there be an outcry against you, that you are not the female we have always professed you to be, but our secret will unhinge each of us from the very persons that might support Elin in her rearing of the child, if the Lord God Almighty allows it to live and be natural.'

'Natural, as in not like me?'

'Yes, child. We will not know if it is the like of you until it is born or even some time after.'

'You said I was all-female at birth?'

'That is so. If you were not, your nature might have been discovered then. It was not until some time passed that your body became confused as to what it should be and only then were you called by a different name for a time.' I did not tell her the name used by her father, for that was not one she would wish to hear.

'Well then, we must hope that the baby does not suffer to be in my like. I think we can all agree on that!'

'Certainly, it has not been easy to keep you hidden, but I do not for a single passing time regret taking you in. You are God-sent to me, Mary, not only as a midwife assistant nor as a companion, but as the gift of a daughter I never had. The first of three blessings Dame Fortune did bestow upon me. It is for that reason that, even if no other but your natural mother and father, and now Mr Brown, suspect your uncommon form, I deeply fear what should happen to you if your disguise is lifted. What if they discovered Mary, the midwife's daughter, is not all she seems? I assure you, you would become as a stranger to them. They would not think you a lamb, but would mistake you for the wolf in lamb's clothing hiding in their midst. They will chase you away. And then my heart would be torn into a million tiny pieces, as would those of Elin and Judith.'

At my admitting my love for her, Mary came once more into my arms and Elin followed. We three held each other for some time in silence, and I contemplated our togetherness and the strength our love gave us.

Then there were four of us. Judith put her arms around the necks of her sisters and myself. When, I pulled back to look at my three daughters, as if of one mind they too drew away. I sought recognition in their eyes that those pillars of strength Mary talked of would be in their understanding we must part.

I was at once dissuaded in my hope by Elin.

'I am glad you have seen our need to be together, Mother. I could not have borne it if you had sent Mary away!'

'You are mistaken, Elin,' I said. 'It is not our strength to keep Mary here that is needed, but our strength to let her go. And that time has come. The coach will soon be ready to leave.'

'No!' Judith cried. She ran to the bed and threw herself face-down upon it and wept.

Mary stepped back from me as if I punched her in the belly. I puzzled at how they had thought anything otherwise than what I meant, but it seemed our purposes had crossed and my intention misunderstood. For a moment she looked to the ground as she so often did. Then reached out and took Elin's hand, freely given. It was as if Elin's strength poured into her as hot iron into a blacksmith's mould and as it filled her it strengthened her.

First she straightened her legs, her back, and then her shoulders until her head came an inch or two above mine. Then she lifted her chin and gained a whole other inch. If ever I saw such determination, it was in a woman determined her man should not go to war, or in the man knowing he must and he may never come back. It was the strength to fight for that one thing neither could imagine losing.

How I envied that purpose. If I could have even a piece of it perhaps I should have more courage.

When she raised her eyes to study me it did not seem as if she knew me at all.

'Mary...' I warned. My voice was borrowed from elsewhere. It was not my own. I could not say more.

That was not a fault in Mary at this time. She still had much to say and she said it forcefully.

'No! No, Mother.' Indeed, if her eyes did not recognise me, neither did I recognise this fierceness in her nature. 'That is no strength, but the cowardly bowing to the bully of common-thinking. You say it must be wrong for us to stay together, but will you admit you played false when all my life you have declared me female? And now I have sired a child, by what measure can you ever believe you played true with me? And will that mistake not be doubly-so for all other persons of this town? If their thinking is nailed down, they can never hold any other belief if all you do is agree with them!'

With renewed breath she continued unchallenged.

'Does any person ever change the belief of another by staying silent or agreeing with them? I can only say how unlikely that is. Indeed, we oftentimes cast our ideas in the wind and hope they are accepted. But if you will look to the farmer, you might gain some wisdom. From him we can learn how he tests whether the ground is good for seed. And if he finds it unwelcoming, he knows the ground will better take the seed if it is first prepared. The best farmer will tell you that it is the hard work in preparing the ground that gives the strongest crop. One must claim the ground, mark the land, plough it, break it, remove the stones, spread muck on it,' she emphasised each task, 'all before the seed is sown, watered, weeded and prayed for. One cannot simply cast the seed to the wind and hope it will grow.'

Mary let go of Elin's hands and threw her arms out at her side to make her point stronger. Even then, I thought she was finished, but she brought to bear the will of that determined farmer and insisted on showing me the idea full-grown.

'Likewise, how can I ever in my life be accepted here if we do not test the ground, prepare it before carefully sowing the seed of acceptance where it might best be grown? Can we not get on our side a few of the best and most clever of persons we can find, and prepare in them compassion toward us?'

It was not Mary that answered to this. It was Elin. She took Mary's hand and squeezed it before coming and taking my own, almost as a joining of the two of us, and fell to her knees. 'Mother, I beg of you, do not send Mary away. Wither she goes, there must I follow, and I do not wish to ever leave you!'

My mother, not being a farmer, knew nothing of preparing ground for seed. Her knowledge was gained by the strife of life. It was she that guided me with the wisdom that a person should hide their differences for, once revealed, they might find themselves hounded to death by those without understanding. Her voice had been strong in me for all my living days and stayed with me still. Yet...

'Sweeting,' I said to Elin, 'I do not want to throw you into despair, but I cannot allow you to go and I cannot allow Mary to stay. We have tarried too long here and the coach will not wait. So, I will say no more upon it.'

'Indeed, you will, Mother.' Mary stepped forward and stood behind Elin still kneeling before me upon the floor. 'Either we both stay or we both go. You cannot make me go, so I choose to stay.

If it does not please you to have me here in this house, then I will have no choice but to find a bed in town. And that will cause those tongues to wag in a way that you nor I will ever be happy about.'

'Believe me, Mother,' Elin declared, 'if Mary must go, I am bound to go with her!'

I pulled my hand free from Elin's. We were undone! My two daughters stood against me. I could not deny Mary spoke rightly. I could not make her go. Neither did I want her to. But if she did not, I did not think they could hide their feelings and then all would be lost.

'Do you refuse me, Mary, even if we are undone? Even if we are made destitute, our clothes threadbare with no bread on our plate, and Elin made to bear the burden of the child alone?' I stepped back away from them. I knew no other argument.

'I will bear the burden if it should come to that.' The voice was so small, yet it was firm. 'I will put bread on the table.' I had forgotten Judith on the bed. That Mary and Elin had also overlooked their younger sister was shown by how startled they were. 'I earn enough of a living for the purpose,' Judith added. Her eyes were swollen by tears and her face marked by being pressed into the blankets.

She did not stand, but her eyes met each of ours in turn, challenging any of us to deny her.

I took my hand-kerchief, dabbed my eyes then waved it before me. With three against me, I could do little but surrender.

Their arguments put me to shame. Where I would put the problem away from myself, my daughters showed me a willingness to stand beside each other even in the face of trouble. Their belief that our love for each other would make us strong enough to shoulder any test we should be put to made me look into my own lack of belief. Even while their loyalty put mine into shadow, doubts of the past came to the fore. Still the lid of that Pandora's box refused to close and sit tight. Despite the battle being lost, I tried one more time.

'Rather you were safe and away from here lest you should

ever be discovered, Mary. And, Elin, you will find yourself the subject of derision for your bastard child. How will you parry the swords drawn against the absent father, whomsoever it is believed he is? Judith, to you I say, what if you should be turned from the plaiting or hat trade for your association with the rest of us and cannot after all earn a living?'

'Mother,' said Elin. 'You seek problems where none yet lie. Let us not conjure them up when others will do that for us. If any should do so, then we will find answers between us. Until then, let us do as you said before and make ourselves acquainted with a suitable story to satisfy any that asks about the child, and let us each know that story so well we are all accountable to it.'

'When, I ask you, did you become so wise, young Elin?' I let go of the fight and allowed myself a smile for the first time that day. 'I will do as you ask of me and I will pray to the Almighty Lord that is acquainted with Lady Fortune to ask her to come and stay with us and keeps us safe.

If God did hear my prayers, He did not answer them and she did not come.

16

Condemnation

'You cannot deny it, Abigale,' said Mrs Jane Wright, her voice both hard as a smith's nail and soft as a milkmaid's butter. She lifted young Charlotte's skirt, the petticoat discarded and folded on the side, and checked how ready the baby was to delivery.

I liked this woman, despite the fact that everything she said might be read as either hard or soft and none would ever know unless she came down on one side or other what her meaning was. There was never a time I did not know her to be anything but what she professed to be, while the inconvenience of not being quite sure of what that was might yet catch one short. Besides, in our younger days we ran together in pigtails.

'Don't expect it's coming for a good few hours.' Mrs Wright lifted the girl's skirt further to expose her low, round belly and rub more of the stone-horse water on it, a thing Charlotte protested strongly over. The noisome smell of piss was not meant as an aid to restoration, something she might find more use for. I did not bring Mrs Wright's attention to this, being used to each other's ways, but made light of it.

'Give her more caudle,' I said. 'Perhaps she will be less complaining.' The women in the room laughed. Charlotte's mother, aunt and sister sat in a circle around her, embroidering the baby blanket they hurried to finish before the baby came. Mrs Wright replaced the skirt over the girl's knees and shifted the girl's feet on the floor to find a firmer position to keep her balance in the wooden birthing chair. We earlier had made merry over her inability to stay still on the chair's small seat, and she had become less steady the more caudle she did drink.

Mrs Wright returned her attention to me. 'It is as I was saying, Abigale, you must tell the magistrate who is the father so he can take the wrong'un to task over it.'

'Impossible.' I did not like to be of no use, so I found some sweet-smelling spices to scatter on the floor around Charlotte to sooth her and build her strength for her travels, which would come soon enough. 'I do not know the man's name, for she has not given it.'

In the adjoining room, Charlotte's brothers and sisters had come home for supper and talked as loud and excitedly as children do. Even the older ones that had spent a day hard at labour, perhaps in the fields, perhaps serving a gentleman of means, made their voices known. Being forbidden, they did not come into the bedchamber, so we carried on as we were, Mrs Wright persisting in her interference about Elin.

'You must make her. If you do not, talk will be as ripe as she is.'

Friend she may be, but that did not challenge her title of meddlesome. As such I warned her, 'It would be less ripe, Jane, if you would be more concerned about this baby's delivery and less concerned about what is not of concern to you.' I used her given name so that I should have her attention, but it was in the manner of having known each other for so many years I spoke to her.

Charlotte's gossips were attentive to all we said, for how else would they be when they were together with us here in Charlotte's bedchamber for the length of her delivery and laying-in? Their needles continued to move and they seemed to look at their stitches as if they thought only of what they did with their hands, but every woman knew it did not take much thought to sew, and entertainment was anything else that happened around them while they did so. I rather it was not the nattering of we two midwives that was so much fair game, so, across the bed, I met the eyes of Mrs Wright and exchanged a whole silent conversation with her, hoping she understood my desire for silence on the topic. She changed the talk to other things for the present.

'I assure you, Abigale, nothing will do but to wait both

patiently and endlessly for this baby to choose when it should come into this world. Perhaps Charlotte has had too much caudle too soon, for it seems she is more than a little asleep!' Charlotte did indeed look too rested to be in the throes and I wondered if it was a false start after all. 'How about some of your recipe? It is sure to do the trick,' she said.

She talked of my treatment, famous for improving how long one must wait for delivery. It might yet aid some movement in this slow time.

Charlotte's gossips sat quiet, apart from the almost silent click-clicking of needles into thimbles. Perhaps they hoped we would talk more on the subject of Elin, since they themselves were not of the most talkative nature. Not in all the time I had been employed by this young women had her women-folk engaged with me in more than a few words. So, we two continued to talk between ourselves.

'She will waken soon enough,' I said. Meanwhile, I removed the things I needed from my bag. Despite earlier heeding my warning, Mrs Wright's curiosity was irrepressible and again she tried to pin the winkle of Elin's secret out of me, speaking in a hoarse whisper rather than full loud at least.

'How will you keep Elin and her baby as well as your other girls? It will surely be a burden for you and I should not like to see you made pauper by her handiwork. You must make her tell you of the father.'

The children in the next room argued over a piece of bread they had found in the pantry and I suggested to their mother she might go out there and tell them to keep their voices low or, if they could not, to go elsewhere. She said she would send them out in the street with a bite to eat. That might keep their mouths busy for a while. And off she went.

Walls were no match for the children's voices and they became louder rather than softer, as did their mother's scolding. Then she sent them outside into the evening air, telling them not to come back before they had learned the value of silence. When she returned, her mood was worse than before and she grumbled there was nobody around to whip the sauciness out of them. One of her older daughters replaced the rug rolled up by the bottom of the door to stop drafts.

'Give her a cup of caudle, Jane,' I said. 'Looks like she has need of it!'

Everybody laughed at that, and a cup was poured for each of us to bring our spirits up. From a leather bag tied with a string I took a handful of different stones and laid them on my palm to see. The light in the room was not much, the curtains having been closed earlier at the start of Charlotte's throes. But the candles danced tall enough, the gaps in windows and the keyhole stuffed with rags so preventing them blowing out or wavering. As well as the candles, light came from the fire burning in the grate to keep mischief away. Sometimes a fog of smoke blew through the room making us cough, likely the result of a wind whipping up outside or a nest stuck in the chimney.

'And where is she today, while you work here?'

'Elin is home resting and taking instruction from Judith on the making of the plait.'

'It is not Elin I ask after but our Mary. I do not believe she has missed a birth unless she was taken to bed with the sickness. Her calm nature is such a blessing to her. Indeed, to all of us in the birthing chamber. And she has such a way with the young ones, keeping them out of mischief when they are such a distraction to the rest of us. We would have none of that noise from those youngsters if she were here. 'Is she unwell?'

'Not at all.' I went on to explain her absence with enthusiasm, the subject of Elin being worn thin. 'Madam Thread-Pecker-' I caught myself in my mistake, being used to calling her by the name Mary and myself had bestowed upon her. 'I am meaning Mistress Cowley. Mistress Cowley busies herself adding the beads to Lady Locklin's evening dress and is given too little time to do it alone and so has requested Mary assist her with the task.' I caught myself speaking too fast and took a breath to slow down. 'Lady Locklin of St Stephens, that is. I am convinced she is better engaged in that than to be here today.

'Indeed?' said Mrs Wright. 'And why are you so convinced, I wonder, when we are in need of her here?'

'We are more than enough–'

'We are short of one to mind the young–'

'She is where she chooses to be.' I did not like to be placed so awkwardly, nor did I wish to go further with this talk. It served no purpose. We were pleased to hear the husband come in from the fields, for now it was for him to look after the children. 'Now, let us apply ourselves to the task at hand and deliver this young woman of her baby.'

Some many hours later, as candle-light drew to a close, we were all a little merrier, and the caudle much lighter in the flask. Charlotte's infant girl had been born in a manner that showed herself to be conducive to an easy delivery and was cleaned, swaddled and suckled. Her mother lay more awake than she should be, laughing and prattling with the rest of us whilst the other women cleaned the floor and made up the bed, and Mrs Wright and myself cleaned and prepared her body for her month-long laying-in.

And then was the time to eat the dainty sugar and almond-paste sweet confections and cakes made into delightful shapes such as pork and crackle farts, trees and flowers and other such things, which were a matter of much discussion and admiration. It mattered less and less what shape they took the more caudle and ale that was drunk and the looser tongues became on matters concerning women.

I stayed long enough to ensure the baby and mother fared well and was pleased to take payment in coins and not in kind. It was well her husband had saved a few. We could not always live off promises. Daylight was nigh on showing its face and fatigue was heavy on my own. Besides, the other women were most of them now sleeping wheresoever they had found a place to sit or lie down.

Mrs Wright, seeing me leave, chose to come through the door with me, so the room could be sealed after us for the rest of the night.

'Tell your Mary she ought come along next time,' she said.

'If she has a mind to learn another trade, I will not stop her.' I could not help but feel I betrayed Mary and pulled the wool over the eyes of my friend, but it was better this way.

'Best tell her she should not have a mind to. Her natural place is by your side and well she must know it.'

'I will not hold her where she does not belong, Jane. She has always had a leaning towards dress-making and she suits it very well. I have released her to follow her own road.' I tried to make lighter of it then. 'I expect she has been snoring a-bed hours ago and will be up and fresh just as I climb under the covers.'

For now, though unhappy to lose a good assistant, Mrs Wright was satisfied by my explanation for Mary's absence and we parted ways. If she was satisfied, it appeared not everyone in that room was equally so, as I was soon to find out.

17

A Warning

'It was not my intention to place further burden upon your shoulders, Mother, when you already walk as if weighed down by shackles. I tell you truly, if I had thought I was doing wrong by answering her, I would not have said a thing. You must know I speak with all sincerity.'

Judith sat on the edge of my rocking chair and leaned forward so that it tipped nearly onto the points of the rockers. She looked as if she would fall out of the seat. I tried to quiet her so that she might tell me what had passed in town to so upset her, but still she balled her fist in her eyes and cried quietly. A teardrop ran down the side of her hand and glistened, somehow catching a glimpse of sunshine even as far from the window as by the hearth.

I had no doubt I was responsible for the guilt my girl was struck by. I had not borne it well after she had told me of her friends' examination of her. She had told them altogether too much of our business... that being the whole of it. Being so, I had let loose all manner of displeasure upon the poor girl. I had sworn at her and cursed her and, to my shame, raised my hand in anger. And, though I did not strike her, my very nearly doing so brought home to me how close I had come to it.

Every part of me trembled. It was clear the day had come when what I most feared had come to pass. And yet, I feared, it was I who brought the pain I had always believed myself the protector against.

I breathed deeply while I gathered together the remaining semblance of motherly nature in me and shaped it back into my own form. It might be too late to have never said harsh words, but perhaps I could take them back and offer some kindness in their stead.

Still, I did not approach my daughter with comfort though I knew I should. While I pulled together more of my shredded feelings, in order to be of use to her in recovering from the blows of my words, she wiped her eyes with the back of her wet hand.

Not taking my eyes from my youngest daughter's downcast head, I forced myself to pay attention to what was before me rather than what was inside of me. I came closer to her and wrung my hands together. Then I clumsily tried to pluck from the air all uncurbed and ill-mannered words I had thrown at her.

'Now, now, girl. What is done cannot be undone.'

The up-shot of my comforting was not at all as beneficial as I had hoped it to be, they not being too comforting, and Judith howled, 'You blame me! You did ride me so hard when I could not know the secret was one until you said so. How should I know? How should I know?' With that, the skinny young girl made more of her remorse than she should instead of aiding me to find a way to undo the mischief. I decided to forgo any further efforts in mending hurt feelings to discover more about our situation.

'Judith. Judith, my child. When you say they are gone to fetch a constable, for what purpose did they go there? Did they mean to arrest a person in this household?'

Judith stopped long enough to nod and say in contradiction to her head's movement, 'I know not, Mother. I did not say it was a constable they went to find. It was not.'

'I must know—' I begun.

'It seems...' Judith stopped to sniff. 'It seems that woman is set on bringing a person by the name of old Mother Fisher that is come from London in order to do something.' Judith's sniffles made it difficult to understand her full meaning.

'Do something?' I said. 'And by 'that woman' I presume you refer to Mrs Brown, who has little better to do with her time than tattle all day long at her garden gate!'

'Yes, Mother. She was as a donkey pulling a cart up a hill, once she started on it. She said to a woman that was visiting with her, Rachel and Norman's Aunt Nora, that she could not believe any of it unless Mary was examined fully both in spirit and body, whatever she meant by that.' Judith again wiped her cheeks with her hands and became thoughtful. 'She was resolved, she did say. She said she would not have amongst us one that was not of God's creatures.'

'We shall see about that. I will not have her besmirching an innocent, especially any daughter of mine.'

'Is it true, Mother? Mrs Brown says, unless the Lord came down among us and chose Elin for immaculate conception, there must be an earthly father for her child. And lest she was mistaken, Elin had not kept company with any but Mary these months, most particularly at the critical time when her seed was ripe for sowing. Then she said, if any man had come through these parts, he must not have stayed long, and unless you were Mother Midnight and Elin a whore, there must be some other puzzle to be solved. And she would be damned to Hell and back if she did not already have suspicions about Mary. What did she mean, Mother?'

There was no use to hiding the truth from Judith now, if she would hear all of it shortly. So, with less misgiving than I should have, and more in the way of making amends for my shoddy treatment of her, I told her. 'Mrs Brown is an interfering so-and-so and should not have said Mary is not one of God's creatures, for every living thing is of His making - every man, woman and child, every grain, animal and tree - and so there is nothing on this Earth that is not his intention and should not be here. Do you understand?'

'Of course. The Lord God made us all. It says so in the song we have often enough sung in a church on Sunday that I cannot be ignorant of it! But why would she think Mary is not of God's making? She is the fairest of all women, the kindest and the cleverest. I do not believe I fully understand what you are saying.'

I could not fault Judith for her innocence, for she was no less a greenhorn than a calf in its first year.

'The reason you do not yet understand is because I have not yet told you anything. Perhaps if you showed some patience, you might piece together what information you can glean from me and then you will know a new thing or two.'

'Yes, Mother. I am at fault. I beg your pardon.'

I thought about what I was to say and how I would say it to one that had no experience as a woman and no knowledge of a man.

'You have taken the bed with your sisters every night since you came here to my house. Is that not so?'

I twisted my hands together. The subject of Mary was not new to me nor one I knew nothing about, but Judith's sweet innocent face, waiting so patient and unknowing for me to cut loose the bond with her sisters, caused me pause for thought. Then again, if she had warning of the names written on the stones that persons might throw at her, she might arm herself with shield and sword against them. Yes, verily it would be a mistake to keep such things to myself, when she would herself hear of them from other places. Though puzzled, Judith nodded to my question. I cleared my throat. 'I must tell you, Judith, this will likely bring you great consternation and a certain amount of dismay and you will not expect the news I must deliver to you.'

'If you talk so wide, it will be a long delivery.'

Like Mary, Judith often revealed herself to be a wit. Though, with her face plain and without any feeling in it, I was unsure of her mood. Perhaps she was funning with me, perhaps she was not, but I felt certain she would not long make a game of it.

'It is now my turn to beg your pardon, Miss, but the tidings you shall have will not be to your liking. I am loath to tell it. Rather would I spare your feelings.'

'Do not be so timid with me, Mother. I am not an unsteady infant wearing a pudding cap and strings. I am a woman living on my own means now.'

If she had long since stopped wearing the commonly worn padded hat, purposed for the stopping of a child bumping its head, and the reins to stop a child wandering off, still she was but a chirpy fledgling not yet ready to fly. I did not say that. Instead I agreed with her.

'Is it not right for a mother to protect her daughter from harm of every sort?' I asked her. 'Aye, but let me tell you what I must without further interruption, and let me tell it to you straight.'

Without further ado I told her of her sisters, watching closely as her mouth and eyes widened. By the time I came to the end of it, she was all mouth and eyes. 'So, there. Your sisters have surprised us and I hope it will not turn you against them. One has got herself with child and the other is neither man nor woman but both. In the books, they call such a one 'hermaphrodite'. I understood from these books that such a one was unable to provide seed, so what has happened here must go against what is common and surprise all of us.'

'Elin's baby's father is a woman? I have never heard of such thing! Surely that cannot be. Is it at all possible?'

'Yes, Judith. It seems that if I did know something of Mary's uncommon form, I did not know everything about it. I did not know her yard was anything but fruitless. I do not know if she is more a woman than a man, or more man than woman, but either way she is enough a man to have sired a child. It does seem I did try and form her into the wrong sex.'

'Is that why you wished to cast Mary out, Mother? Must we do so? It seems as if that is the same as crossing to the other side of the road when we should be the Samaritan.'

'Nay, I am not so strong on that as I was. I cannot cast either out, but it might be that I must yet send them to London awhile to stay with some suitable persons I know.' It irked me somewhat that my first thought was to protect ourselves when Judith's first thoughts were for her sisters. Where her age was such that she might not show consideration for others, my very occupation should have had me doing so. I tried to save face as well as I could. 'They are family, Judith, part of our household flock. We cannot change their form or that they strayed, but we are not after all obliged to throw them to the wolves to save ourselves.'

It seemed Judith was not listening.

'Hark, Mother. What noise is that? Does a procession come down our street?' She moved over to the window and peered out.

'I am certain there is not,' I said. I stilled myself to listen. From the rising gabble of approaching voices, I might be wrong.

The approaching voices were several, both young and old.

Amongst the voices, were some of women I knew and some I did not. From which direction they came, I knew not, but their voices gained strength the closer they came and it was likely they came from the town. I could not think where else. One stood out in particular, the frailer tone of an accent found more commonly in the city. From the others, the general babble, I cleanly plucked one or two snippets, an easy task when none of them pretended any kind of secrecy or subtlety.

'… at my last three and that of my eldest…' came one.

'If… as Mrs Brown suspects, …call her a she or an it?' came another

'…not a she, but an it!' The unmistakable voice of Mrs Brown.

'If this is true, she - it - has attended two of my laying-ins…'

'We are all duped!'

'Indeed. Have they not all of them hoodwinked us?'

'Aye, we are fools to them…'

I caught more full sentences the closer they came. I heard enough to know there was not a single kindly voice among those coming toward us. Certainly, none friendly toward Mary nor myself. I wiped my hands on my apron. If I had been waiting for this moment all day, I had been waiting twenty-one years and more. Never would I be ready, but if I could be, I was as ready as I had ever been.

'Judith?' She barely gave me her attention as she pulled aside the curtain to peer out. 'Judith. You must go before they get here. Go out the back door.'

'They are upon us. I will not leave you alone when they outnumber you ten to one.'

''Tis not me they come for but Mary.'

'That is not what I hear.'

I went to the other side of the window next to Judith and

I, too, pulled back the curtain to better see who was there. It was not my intention to draw attention to myself, but I could not see through the dirt, so I rubbed a small clear circle with the side of my fist. The cool glass blackened my hand. Even now, they were already at the door, perhaps deciding who should knock.

Pressing my face close to the pane, I could only see the sides and backs of those following at the rear. I bumped my forehead trying to put my eyes on the other side of the glass. Someone must have heard the noise, for several of the women turned to the window and Mrs Parks, the mother of those two busy-body children Rachel and Norman Parks, that went to plaiting school with Judith, did point and say out loud, 'There she is! Old Mother Harris will know where the creature hides herself, or where she does herself hide her.'

I can say now how that had me incensed. So much so that I was impelled to open the window before even I had thought of the outcome of my actions. I should instead have bolted the door. Straight away, more than ten women stood around the window, and one that I thought might be Mrs Goody Bassett's daughter took hold of the window and pulled it wide.

'There you are, my dear Mrs Harris. We have come… Indeed, it may be you know the reason for our visit, and I warn you most strongly we do not stand on social occasion.'

The town's biggest tattler, the wife of Mr Brown the baker, wore the satisfactions of one who was at last proved right after years confiding in her husband all her suspicions, only to be told to 'mind only our business, dear, and not that of every other person in town'. It was a look that fit her well, but did not suit her at all. That she enjoyed her position as the head of the mob was all too obvious.

'Mrs Brown. I wonder at your triumph. The Lord might consider the attention you are enjoying to be quite unbecoming. You should be warned not to take too much pride in your good self. It is not I who will judge you, but judgement comes to each of us at the end.'

If I thought to prick the air out of her puffed-up feathers, I was mistaken in it. She raised her brows and half closed her eyes, while still keeping the satisfaction in her smile.

'Now, now, Abigale,' she said. 'We are not come to see you, though it will be in your greatest interest to stay. We are here to see that one you call Mary. The one you most maliciously and falsely disguise as a woman to trick us all. One we have accepted into our midst for nigh on twenty-two years as your daughter…'

'One we have more than accepted in our midst!' The woman that I thought might be Mrs Bassett's daughter poked her finger at my face, and it took every piece of patience to not to bite it or hit it away. 'We have welcomed it - that creature - into our birthing chambers. Many-a-good-woman has accepted her - it - at her laying-in where no man is so welcomed. You, Mrs Harris, have tricked us into taking her amongst us as a viper into our nest.'

'I do beg your pardon, Miss. Are we acquainted?' I did not like to be addressed in such a way by a person not introduced to me, especially one so young and not much older than my daughters.

'Whether we are or we are not is of no concern here. For the matter we have come to address today, I know enough of it for this to be of interest to me. If I had myself unknowingly welcomed a man into my bed chamber when I was confined, I would feel myself to be most forcefully hoodwinked and shamed.'

'Well then, Miss, since it is nothing to you except in possibility, I suggest you stay out of it. There are no men in my house.' I know not if I impressed them with my calm as I meant to, but it was at least pleasing to place one of them in their rightful place.

My crowing over the young woman no better than Mrs Brown's over me, I pulled myself up and turned my attention to the older woman. Though by her nature she was small, in the midst of every other woman squeezed round her, she seemed contrarily to be both shrunken and enlarged by them. Shrunken by their height, yet enlarged by their numbers.

Her years were plenty and had marked her thin and craggy face with apparent wisdom. And it was to her wisdom the good women of St. Albans had presumably confided, and in that same wisdom I must also place my trust, for I had no other place to turn with Mary and Elin soon to come back home, and I had no wish for them to be challenged in the street.

Behind the old woman, the other women talked loudly amongst themselves in a way that was most unflattering to myself and my family

'I will not have you all inside, but I see I must talk with one of you. Who will it be?' I now pretended ignorance of the old woman's importance and took my time to look each of them in the eye with the hope that I gave Judith time enough to get away to find Mary and Elin. I settled on the old woman. 'I think you have travelled great distance to see me, madam? You must be in need of refreshment. I will talk to you over a cup of something.'

The woman I spoke to might be old, but I was convinced her mind was as sharp as her eyes and took in everything. She nodded, but said nothing. Her eyes stayed on mine without sway.

I bobbed my head and told the old woman that I would open the door if she would care to use that rather than the window to talk to me, but again said that I had no wish to talk to anyone else.

'Do you think we are here to wait outside? If that is so, you are very much mistaken, Mrs Harris,' one woman said. I ignored her. It was my house and I would not have all these people inside.

'Judith.' I whispered as I turned from the window, taking her hand and pulling her toward the door with me. She had not moved. 'Go now and warn Mary and Elin to stay away. I will keep these women here.'

'Mother,' she whispered back. 'If they will be judged, what is the worst sentence that can be laid upon them? They have done no crime. They are not criminals. Would it not be better to have done with it now than later?'

'No, it would not, Judith. Do as I have told you. Now!'

Reluctant to leave, Judith went slower than I would have liked toward the back door. She grabbed up her boots and pulled them on without fastening the laces.

As soon as she closed the door behind her, I took off my

apron and smoothed down my dress. Then I drew a deep breath and released it in readiness to face the angry women.

I opened the front door.

'Would you care to come in?' I said only to the old woman, who had not yet moved. When she nodded again, I stood aside and opened the door wider.

No sooner than I did so, all the other women crowded around the old woman and, squeezing together as they crossed over the threshold, passed through the doorway as one overly large woman, much of her being made up of Mrs Brown. I tried to stop them by closing the door, pretending not to see them coming, but it was a task as impossible as stopping the wind. They merely pushed open the door and in they came. And, as one, they gathered their dresses and bustled over to the unlit fireplace.

Not a single one of them thought to take off their boots or beg pardon for not doing so and, with them, they carried the stinking muck of the street and covered the floor with it. They trampled mud into Judith's straw that she had been working on..

There were too many to offer a seat, even if I had a wish to, so I offered up my rocking chair to the old woman, who had yet to introduce herself. She held out the twist of wood she used as a walking stick to one of the nearby women, who took it, then sat.

'Madam,' I said. 'You have the advantage over me. I think you must know who I am, but I am as yet at a loss to know your name or your reason for being here.'

'I am Mrs Elizabeth Fisher, senior midwife of Ludgate Hill in London, and I am called upon to assist yourself and your sisters of St. Albans to determine what to do about the creature in your midst.'

'There is no 'creature' here, only myself and my three children.'

'Now that is the very thing I am here to discover. These womenfolk have brought to my notice a predicament that unsettles them immensely. There has been much chatter over this, and it is incumbent on me to put an end to that chatter and see to it that every person with an interest in it is satisfied. It is to do with the nature of the one you call your daughter.'

'And what gives rise to your suspicion that everything is not satisfactory with my daughters? They are fine young women. Their goodness and Godly upbringing cannot be in question. You cannot find false their piety, their manners nor any other thing about them.'

Already I had made up my mind that I would not after all offer refreshment. I could not bear to make welcome a person that was here to judge those I held so dear to my heart.

'Now, Abigale. We are not questioning their goodness, only whether or not one of them, that has 'til this time been asked and welcomed into the birthing chamber, should be allowed such privilege.' Mrs Brown placed herself to the side of old Mrs Fisher to borrow some of her authority. 'If it is true, and we are convinced it must be so, that Mary is not as she seems but is in fact not the woman we have always believed her to be, then we must discover this for ourselves and decide what is to be done about it.'

I was not in a position to remove her self-righteous demeanor, but only to defend my children.

'There is nothing you need do about it, Mrs Brown. My daughters are all they have ever been, and you have known Mary her whole life. Has she ever behaved in a way you or any other might call offensive? Never! Has she done anything other than that of every other daughter in the town? Nay, she has not. She has always been admirable for her caring and helpful nature. She is of the gentlest disposition and has shown dedication to becoming a most excellent midwife. Never, not once, has there been any complaint about her. She has conducted herself in a manner above question, so how can anything else be of importance?'

I balled my fists and tried to show how indignant I was over any of my children being quizzed, but all my bluster did was mark my dress with the dirt from the window that before marked the side of my hand.

Before even we could talk further upon this matter, to my dismay Mary and Elin came in the front door, talking fast between them as was their wont, and giggling as two mischievous girls hanging on the apron strings. It was a great misfortune that Judith must have missed giving them my warning.

Seeing the group of townswomen surrounding the old woman in the rocking chair by the fireplace, Mary stopped abruptly. Her mouth dropped and the blood left her cheeks.

'Mother?'

18

Mrs Elizabeth Fisher

'Mother?' Mary repeated her question.

'What—?' Elin remarked, having come after Mary into the room and belatedly perceived us standing there. When she stopped, she dropped some flowers she had been holding. Daisies. Always daisies, I remembered from the past. Around both their necks and wrists were daisy-chains, telling very clearly how they had passed the time since this morning. To those that looked on, perhaps mostly to me, the two of them looked together as any other two adoring sisters might, except for the ripe mound of Elin's belly.

'Mary, Elin, this is Mrs Fisher from London.' I gestured toward the old woman, who did not stand up in acknowledgement of my daughters. Given her age and theirs, I was neither surprised nor offended. 'She is here to see you.'

While I made the introduction, I tried to plan how to send the two away, but could think of no reason good enough that would not raise suspicion. And where would they go? Even if they found a place, they would at some time be obliged to return. Perhaps I could rid the house of these women before then. My mother's face came to mind again. 'What the townswomen think will make you or break you,' she had said. It gave me more pause than I wished for.

Recognising the respect the old woman obviously commanded, Mary, then Elin, curtsied and said, 'Good day to you, ma'am.'

The woman waved her dried-up hand and studied the girls. 'Which of you has the yard?' Both Mary and Elin blushed and lowered their gaze. Dismissing Elin with 'It is apparent it cannot be you', she turned her attention to Mary. 'You do not have the appearance of a man.'

'I am not, Ma'am.' She kept her head low.

'Have you the tools of a man?' Mrs Fisher was direct in her asking.

Mary's face blanched but she did not answer. Neither did I expect her to. This was the question we had lived in dread of hearing for the whole of her life. And now it was here, and we were so close to discovery, I found the nearness of it did not bring any relief. I looked to the door to see if there was any way we could escape, but there was none. Nor could I think of anything that might give us time to find another way.

'Answer her, Mary.' Mrs Brown seemed to speak for all the women there. Now I looked at them, I saw some faces of women I had birthed. Mary also. They were not so strong in their confrontation as Mrs Brown, standing quietly and watching rather than encouraging the two leaders forward. It seemed, then, that Mrs Brown led the way against Mary. I should not be surprised and I would never forget her betrayal. Unless it was her husband that had betrayed us. No, that did not figure. My trust in him was complete.

'You are not obliged to answer to them, Mary,' I said. 'You are not on trial.'

Nevertheless, Mary answered.

'What will you have me say?' Like a river, the blood flowed in a rush back to her face, flushing the white from her cheeks and leaving them burning as a glowing ember. Sweat covering her skin. My heart cracked for my little girl, the happy child she was before she understood how she was different from her sisters, taking that vitality from her.

Into my mind came a picture of her coming in from the fields between the house and the Ten Man Ditch where she played, covered in daisy chains very much as today. In that moment, I saw how she had shared so much time with Elin as they grew. From there, I saw in my mind's eye, time after time, that quiet but content little girl smiling the biggest smile at so many persons in the town, some of the women being in this room. Even as a growing woman, when she had reigned in her childhood exuberance, she was known to often share her good nature with any with whom she talked, both within the laying-in chambers and without.

I felt shame then. For years, as was done to me, I had made this young child keep a secret, the secret of her body, not for her sakes but for my own. I had not considered how my own prejudice forced that happy child to hide herself. I had to defend that child, now full grown.

'Leave her be, Mrs Fisher.' The old woman, used to being listened to and obeyed, was taken aback for being talked to in that way by me. 'I have something to say.'

'No, Mrs Harris. It is I that have something to say.' Though small, the old woman commanded obedience. Even I, that was my own mistress for nigh on thirty years or more, and with so much to say on the matter, closed my mouth and listened.

She placed her hands on the arms of the rocking chair and, with the assistance of two other women taking her elbows, pushed herself to standing. The chair tipped dangerously forward, so I thought she might fall out of it and perhaps hit her face on the stone hearth. Did I wish it? Nay, that would be ungodly of me.

Once to her feet, the woman that held her twisted piece of stick returned it to her. She shuffled before Mary and Elin, both of whom faced the floor with their hands clasped together.

'If I am to be a judge in this, I must know all there is to know.' The old woman stood shaky before Mary. 'Tell me, Mary, if that be your name, did you lie with your sister and make her with-child as is talked of here?'

Mary lifted her eyes, though not her head. Her words belied her shame as if she had none. 'I did, though she is not in truth my sister by blood, and it was right I should do so when my love for her was so strong I could resist it no longer. But it was not my intention. It was Eros who did guide us there to that place.'

If she had intended to prevent further speculation by her

confession, she was mistaken in that. Neither did it stop the condemnation of the visitors.

'Well I never did. No shame,' said one of the women.

'Scandalous!' said another.

'I cannot credit it,' said a third.

'Intention or not, it is my belief you did this girl wrong by acting on your windy member.' Mrs Fisher smacked her lips together while she thought.

The other women murmured and exclaimed with no thought to holding their thoughts to themselves.

'Have her prove it,' said one, grabbing each side of her skirt and tugging it down with determination. 'Mary is no more a man than I. She covers for the true father.'

'Nay, 'tis not likely she would construct a story so wild and unbelievable if it were not so.'

If my body was tight wound as a clock spring before, now it screamed to seek release. Why did I then hesitate when I was her only hope for defence? I had my answer. A lifetime of fear instilled in me by my mother and my own imaginings.

Elin had remained silent until this moment. Now she too raised her eyes, finding the one accusing her beloved Mary of covering for the father. In the same way as her sister had surprised me with her forcefulness, so then did Elin.

'Do not doubt what she says. She speaks true. Our affection has been great since… forever. When Eros took aim and pierced the hearts of the both of us with a single arrow, only then did we seal our affection with a kiss.'

Some women snickered.

'Takes more 'n a kiss to make a baby, girl.'

When Mrs Brown furrowed her brows, I readied myself for another barb. Still I could not think how to defend my daughter. I should have thrown every one of these women into the street, but I could neither speak nor move, the whole of me wrapped in foreboding.

'This is no matter for amusement, ladies. These two present a serious problem. One might have tricked us all her life, the other is with-child and proves no father to us.' Mrs Brown rebuked them.

There I was forced to at least try to refute our busy-body neighbour. And once I began, my words were a waterfall that could not be dammed.

'Do not dare lay the secrecy of this at any child's door! How can you blame a daughter for following the instruction of her mother? If you must lay blame thickly upon anyone, you must paint me with it. My girls are good and obedient and have only done as I have told them. If it is something I have done, only I am responsible for pulling the hood over your eyes and keeping you in the dark. If Mary's nature was known to you, would you have welcomed her and accepted her as you have done all these years, or would you have made a mockery and a sideshow of her? She is my daughter and I love her as I love each of my children and as any mother should. Would you have me betray them to a lifetime of unhappiness? Would you set their place outside society? Mary is everything a daughter should be. She is kind and attentive. She is dutiful and loving. She has learned a calling so that she may earn a living for herself and provide toward the household. Do not dare accuse her of anything, for she is innocent in all this!'

Having spoken without pause for some minutes, when I stopped, the women stared at me with astonishment. When none spoke, I added, 'Do not make Mary carry this cross. 'Tis mine to bear.'

Then Mrs Fisher, that had not taken her eyes from Mary the whole time I spoke, thrice banged her twisted branch on the timbers of the floor, making the house shudder and shake. Her quiet but imperious voice commanded attendance upon her.

'First, we must prove what you say is true. The people of the town who know this one,' she pointed her forefinger at Mary's chest, 'are not so convinced it is not now they are being hoodwinked rather than before, though one cannot find good reason to think you would conjure such excuse out of nothing. However, one way or the other, considering the importance of such deception, whether it is before or now, I will discover it.'

'I tell you,' I said, 'I cloaked Mary's true nature for the love of a mother for her child, but now her true nature is fully revealed and needs no further examination.'

'And I tell you, I will examine the one you cast as female, to discover any and all truth that might remain hidden.'

'To what end would you do so?' I placed myself between the woman and my children.

'She has attended many a laying-in, is this not so?'

'She will not do so again, for it would not be right–'

The old woman interrupted.

'It was not right before.'

'I have that knowledge now, but did not before fully understand–'

Again, she did not let me finish.

'That cannot be true. You know as well as, or more than, any a man is not welcome in that most closed and sacred of places.'

'Mary was never a man. Rather, I did not know her complete design until lately, and then I have no longer allowed her there.'

The old woman looked at the other women to the left and right of me, enjoying the excitement, and singled out those closest to Mary with her eyes. 'You, aye you, get that one,' she pointed at Mary with her free hand, 'and bring her to me. You there and you, hold this one still.' She nodded her head toward me.

Before I realised I was already held and trapped, I tried to go to Mary. I had left it too late. Elin gasped and covered her mouth with both her hands. Mary stepped back a pace from the woman. Then took another toward the door. Two of the women by the fireplace broke off from the group and with a 'She tries to run!' came between Mary and the only escape she might have reached.

'Be still, creature! Whether you will be examined willingly or not, you will lift your skirt and show us what you hide there.'

That it was our neighbour, Mrs Brown, that was so zealous in exposing Mary was of no surprise but much disappointment. Her good husband, with whom I had passed so many early morning hours, spoke too often of her graces: her goodness and her charity, her sense of duty to God, the Church and those less needy than ourselves. His praise could not have been stronger or fonder. Yet here she was, the fiercest against Mary with no thought to the delicacy of her feelings or mine. Worse, she led others that might be Mary's friend against her.

'Mrs Brown, take heed. That is my child to whom you speak.' I tried and failed to pull free from two sets of hands holding me. 'Even I would not presume to command her to reveal herself. She is of age, and if she chooses to keep herself private, by what right do you seek to violate that privacy? You are not a judge, a jury nor an alderman. You are not any kind of lawman.'

Old Mrs Fisher licked her lips before she spoke. 'Mrs Harris. Perhaps you care to take yourself and your girl here,' she gestured toward Elin, 'outside while we do what is necessary? Perhaps you will wish to spare yourself and your daughter? We are here to examine this other one and we will not leave until we have done so.'

'Again I say, by what right do you order me and my family in my own home? You are not my husband or father, and you are not a justice or a constable or judge representing the King's law. We are free women and may do as we please.'

'Do as you please, by all means, but it is you that did bring this one into the laying-in chamber. The women she helped deliver, as well as any she might have attended in the future, will wish to know who comes to their bedside.' The old woman held up her scolding finger. 'If you must talk of rights, then I defend the right of such mothers and protect them in their right to know if male or female is in attendance upon them at such a time when men are unwelcome.'

Even not liking it, I saw the sense she made. Still with the intention of saving Mary from further shame, I came back with, 'What if I were to give surety that Mary will never again attend a birth unless she is invited? I assure you, she will no longer be my deputy, for she shall make her own way as a seamstress. As neither judge nor constable, that must be good enough for you.'

'You show great stubbornness, Mrs Harris. Again I ask you to avail yourself of our goodwill and take your daughter outside. For your defence of your child, I commend you, but for your standing in the path of justice for those whose privacy has already been violated, I demand you step back and let us do what is necessary.'

The women behind Mary stood fast on the way to the door. Even if she ran, she could not escape. Again, I ask, where would she go? She had no place to hide herself and they only had to await her return.

Her eyes pleaded with me. They were as of an animal set for slaughter. I had seen it on many a market day. I tried to reach out my hand to her but my arms were held. And, as she raised hers toward mine, the old woman lifted her stick and brought it down sharply on her arm. Mary clasped her arm where it was rapped close to her chest, bending over it. She was full of pain.

Attacked thus, Mary rightly defended herself. Gone was her servitude. Gone was her meekness and shyness. Her face blazed red. Her eyes stood wide with shock, wet in the corner where, unnoticed, she had shed a tear, she leaned forward and grabbed the weapon that was used against her.

The moment she moved, it was as if all others in the room were released from those dull bonds of stupor. The shouts of all the women came at once.

'Grab her!' one cried out.

'She attacks Mrs Fisher,' said another.

'The creature tries to break loose!' yelled a third.

Elin ducked out of the way as Mary raised the stick above her head beyond the reach of the old woman reaching high to grab it back. Her very raising of it gave rise to further outcry.

'She attacks the elder!'

'Look out. She tries to kill her!'

Though Mary acted to resist attack as every person has a right to do, they only took notice of how she waved that stick above her head.

'Leave her be. She does nothing but defend herself.' That was Elin.

With everybody shouting and the women gathering around Mary just beyond the reach of the stick, I could not clearly see her. Not helping her case, she waved that stick threateningly at the crowd around her. She was as a baited badger cornered by a snarling dog. I had oftentimes seen such shows in the market. I understood her fear, but her actions spoke against her. Even the women who had earlier stood back undecided now came down on the side of calling her 'monster'.

'Watch out. She has gone mad! Take the stick from her.'

Elin moved away from grabbing hands with her own hands protecting her belly.

'Mary, give her the stick,' I said. So intent on keeping the women away from her, Mary did not hear me. 'Mary! Give it to her!'

This time, in between waving around the stick, Mary looked to me, but I saw she did not know what I asked of her. There was no understanding in her face, only fear and confusion. If ever I did see one who had lost her place in the world, it was Mary, here, now. And was it not I to blame for the losing of it?

If I had not forced her to keep my secret, this would never have happened.

If I had not taken her with me into the birthing chamber, they would never have had reason nor excuse to interfere where they had no business.

And if I had been stronger in sending her to the city, perhaps I could have averted her plight and even now she would be safe.

'Mary! Give her the stick, Mary. They do not come to hurt you.' Did I add a further lie to my nest of them? I went to take the stick before they hurt her in the gaining of it, but again I was held fast. She turned around, still waving it in all directions.

'I have done nothing, mother. I have done nothing. I am innocent in all this. Why do they attack me so? Why do they seek to take my dignity?'

In her question was truly her innocence. She had never understood what I had for years dreaded. It was there in her eyes that she never truly believed any would hold her sex against her. It was likely she would never comprehend how her business was anything to do with anyone but herself and Elin.

'Mary, give me the stick. You make the matter worse for yourself.'

Old Mrs Fisher reached out to take it. Mary held it back over her head out of reach and one of the women behind her grabbed it. A big woman passed the offending item back to Mrs Fisher, who took it and immediately banged it again on the floor.

All of a sudden, with Mary's defences down, like a pack of dogs on that poor badger, the women surrounded her. They grabbed her and held her arms behind her back. Our home, our place of refuge, had become a place of cruel torment. The silent tear that had earlier held her lashes was joined by others, even as she still struggled. Elin too was crying. It was hard for me not to join them. If I could have sent Elin away out of there then and spared her as the old woman had suggested, even when I could not - would not - myself leave, I would have done so. But it was too late.

'Lift her skirt and let us see what secret she hides from us.' The old woman, once more in charge of her stick, was also once more imperious in her demand.

19

Examination

Mary cried out. And she fought them as best she was able. She could not easily give but a token struggle, for there were too many holding her now.

Too many.

Elin stood back. She held her belly with one hand. She would defend Mary if it were not for that she would place her baby, their baby, in danger. And in any case, there was nothing to be done against so many.

What kind of mother was I to allow these women have their head over me? What manner of woman was I that would let them shame my daughter so? Furthermore, where was my courage to face down these women that came into my house and treated Mary so crudely? Tears fell inside my heart for the sham-mother I had become. Again I tried with words.

'I demand you stop. You have no right to come into my home and brow-beat us so! Out! Out now! I shall call the constable.' I breathed heavily, my defence of Mary too small and helpless. I might not be as old as Mrs Fisher, but my bones were weak enough with age to make me feeble against the younger women.

'Still yourself, Mrs Harris. We will not hurt the creature, only satisfy ourselves as to its nature.'

Held as I was, I pleaded with all my heart.

'May the Lord Almighty forgive you! Stop! Mary is not a creature, not an 'it'. She has lived the life as a woman and is one in nearly every sense you can think of. You all know how gentle and kind she is, and how she has helped so many, not only in the birthing chamber, but she gives her kindness freely to any that needs it. Do not demean her by taking from her the thing that makes her a woman. She is no animal. She is my daughter.'

Even as I appealed to them to go no further, Mrs Brown pushed forward a woman I knew of by face but not by name as one who had attended Charlotte's laying-in. She did not appear to be at all comfortable with the role into which she had been cast, but the nature of a person is such that she will rarely stand up to a browbeater unless her fear of doing so is greater than that of the bully. I beseeched her to have mercy. Her eyes met mine and I knew the reason for her hesitation was our knowing each other and passing time together.

Not so the town washer-woman, who passed her by. This was the one with not a bit of meat on her bones and a reputation for cleaning the inns' sheets after farmers and passing merchants had left their stains on them. I had little to do with her except nodding to her on occasion, on account of her being Elin's mistress, and perhaps bidding her good day as she beat the clothes and sheets on the stones. She did not have the first woman's qualms. Already she was bending to lift Mary's skirt.

'How can you think to do this? You have children. Think. If it were your child, would you treat her so shabbily?'

She did not hesitate.

Mary's face.

I would never forget it.

The way her eyes rolled back and showed more white than colour brought to mind that baited bull, or a hog fleeing for its life. Her shame was my shame.

If a man or men had violated her, worse could not have been done to her than by these woman. I saw no difference in what they did and what a man did when he held a woman down and took her against her will.

'Mother!' Her eyes, her body, her voice beseeched me. It was all I could do to not cry with her. Outwardly, I failed in that too. Inside, I cried as if the Heavens themselves had opened. 'Mother. I

150

beg thee, please no.'

'No! No! Have mercy.' My throat was dry and the words came as a loud growl. I could move no more than she. 'Do not defile her. Leave her be, you... you beasts!'

My poor daughter.

'Hush now, Mrs Harris. You make too much fuss of it. It will be but a quick examination. No more is necessary. We will only know if it is a male or female, then we will be done.'

I curled my fingers into my palm, and if I could have reached Mrs Brown, I would have slapped her for the indignity she put Mary to.

'It matters not how fast you violate a person, when 'tis the action of violation that is in question. Do not make yourself a party to this.'

'Nonsense, Abigale. We have no intention to harm Mary. We come here only to discover the truth.'

If they believed that, their sensibilities must be stunted. The harm they did was deeper than they could imagine.

Even as the washer-woman took hold of the hem of Mary's dress, Mary pulled her arms in front of her and held them down toward her knees to stop them lifting her skirt.

Her legs bent under her and I thought she would fall to the ground, but they held her up. And they took hold of her hands and held them to the side so the washer-woman had no obstruction. When she lifted the fabric, the pain that was Mary's was mine also. So clear was my mother's warnings not to trust any with my secret. Stabbed by betrayal of those we had known so long, my heart broke and bled all over the place. Right beside Mary's.

To poor Mary's mortification, every woman in that room laid eyes upon her that day. I too could not help but glimpse beneath her dress. A thing I did not need to do, for as her mother I knew enough to guess what lay there. Nevertheless, even if it was not my business more than of any other, I was curious. Indeed, what I saw surprised me, for she had turned more man than woman, and I had not known it after all. I had imagined her privates to be somewhat riper than when I last saw them, before she came to the age of change, but here was something comparable to a maturing boy. By wrapping Mary in a woman's dress, I had confined a youth in a woman's gaol. But none of this was my will alone.

'I cannot fathom it. There is Rogero. And there is the cleft. I have never seen such thing.' The washer-woman could not have been more astonished. 'Nay, I never did.'

'Take your face out of that creature's privates and let us take a peep.' Even the two holding me loosed their hold and leaned forward to see Mary below the waist. 'Aye, there they are, Mercury and Venus in bed together.'

'Hold your tongue, woman,' I said. I never before was so filled with anger at any person. 'Do not make a freak of her. She is a good girl.'

Leaning in to better see, Mrs Brown laughed. 'A girl it is not. It is neither. And both. But not one or the other, Mrs Harris. You have thrown a dark veil of secrecy over this one's yard and fooled us all with your trickery. Now stand aside and let us do what we must do.'

Each took their turn to look and exclaim such as, 'What is that?', 'Mary is misnamed' and 'By the name of Hermaphrodites…'

I pulled free my loosened arm from one of the women's hold and grabbed at Mrs Brown's sleeve, wishing to bring her attention back to me. She turned on me then, eyes fierce. Her thinned and pursed lips scarce moved across her teeth in her set jaw. As she spoke, she approached me one small step at the time, slow and deliberate. Despite my advantage of being taller than the woman, I admit to my broken heart finding enough life to beat me back a pace or two. I did think she would attack my body and squeaked even as her words came like bullets at me.

'Do not come the high one in this, Mrs Harris. You have hidden a curiosity here in our peaceful town. You have deliberately, maliciously and completely deceived us. You forfeit your right to have a say in any of this. Do not tell us what to do. Do not tell us anything, for none will trust any word you utter for the rest of your life!'

'I did only what any mother would do for the sake of her child.' My own eyes pricked with the salt of my shame, for Mrs Brown was right. I had done this to my Mary and I had fooled my fellow men and women. 'You must not punish Mary for what I have done!'

'Silence, woman. I am not yet decided what punishment will suit. I am thinking on it, Mrs Harris.' Mrs Fisher shuffled to the fireplace and sat on my chair frowning. She did so without her stick, any support or request for it.

Some time had passed and Mary, now released, embraced Elin close together by the fire-side where the other women had so recently stood. I stood before my girls holding a fire-iron, defending them too late. The towns-women stood around us talking amongst themselves. Old Mrs Fisher had been silent for some time, her eyes closed, perhaps in prayer or perhaps asleep. None thought to disturb her or perhaps didn't dare.

Then she spoke, still with her eyes closed, knowing we were waiting for her to talk and so would listen. She was not mistaken.

'If the Lord has seen fit to create a person in Mary's form, then who are we to judge Him? He makes no mistakes.'

Mrs Fisher's next words, where she invited us to deliberate the worthiness of every living creature and defend against any accusation made against it, destroyed the argument I had prepared by its very agreement to it.

Mrs Brown, of course, did not agree.

'What of rats and fleas? Are they God's—'

Mrs Fisher opened her eyes and spoke loud and sharp over Mrs Brown's words.

'Enough.' The old woman banged down her twisted stick hard on the floor with more strength than I would credit her. Even with her sitting, and with so many standing upon the floor, still she was able to cause the floor to shake. 'Enough I say.' This time her eyes silenced Mrs Brown and left her words hanging. 'I have sought the word of the Lord and have been blessed with an answer. We will go to the judge and have him decide.'

20

A Gentle Husband

The Justice, that was an Alderman and at some times the Mayor, sometimes the Farmer of Excise, and sometimes Commissioner for Assessment, sat behind his large oak table at the back of the room that served as both court and meeting room in the Town Hall.

Though Mr Justice Gape had known we women were there for some good fifteen minutes, it being market day his attention was almost wholly upon the few men coming and going and none at all upon us.

There was the clerk carrying some papers, and there were some men with their hands waving at each other and the Justice trying to placate them. Behind them, also waiting his attendance upon them, were divers other persons fresh covered in mud and muck from the pigs or cows they had driven into town.

It seemed the Justice would have little time to see us today, but it was equally certain that Mrs Fisher, Mrs Brown and the other women would not leave until he had. In the meantime, our disagreements plodded on in timely fashion, not caring that the one that should hear them had yet to lend us his ears.

'You cannot lay blame on one that had no say in their destiny,' I said. 'It was I that sought God's will in deep prayer. And it was in answer to that prayer the Almighty let his perfect will be known that I should raise his child this way.'

Rather would I have had the Justice, that would decide Mary's fate, hear what I wished to say, but I must stand beside Mary against the harsh accusations of these women. These women that once accepted us. I had need of that same acceptance now.

'Chosen? By what standard do you say such creature should compare? God did say in the Bible...'

Mistress Cowley failed to finish the sentence when others looked to her to hear what she had to say about her apprentice. When had she joined our party? As usual, she bobbed her head, though without needle or thread in her hand, she appeared to merely peck without forming exquisite stitches. If she wished to piece together a battle of knowledge, I believe I could stitch together a fairer argument on that.

And if she must bring God's Will into question, she could not know more than I on this subject, when I had passed many an hour studying the words of the Good Book as so many of intelligent nature did. None could examine my knowledge of it without seeing how prepared I was for this. On this, I could speak with strength.

'Every child descended from Noah and his ancestor Adam is God's child. That is a thing you cannot question-'

'God would not create such abomination!'

'Think you that a child can be born that God did not know of and have a hand in?' I straightaway had my answers. 'Do you question the Will of God, when He has given us so many divers children to welcome among us? Every child is God's creation, do you not agree?' I did not await an answer. 'Then, if God chooses to enjoy such diversity, who are we to condemn his creation!'

Of course, Mrs Brown must have her say as well.

'It is not God's will but that of the other one you have, Abigale. You have the ear of the Devil. This creature you call your daughter, it should be destroyed or cast out.'

This drew gasps from all those that stood around us listening to our arguments. That they did not immediately side for Mary's downfall was a thing I must celebrate and make use of.

'Nay, it is you that is mistaken, Mabel for, as you did admit, God does not make mistakes and if He has breathed life into any single living creature, He intends a path for that creature we mortals cannot know. It is not our place to question, only to accept. Furthermore, Mabel, if God can see the beauty and love in every one of His creations, then who are we lowly mortals to say otherwise? I am certain it is His will we love every one of his children equally.'

With that, Mrs Brown became triumphant.

'The Lord tells us there are two sexes, Abigale. Two. Adam and Eve. Man and woman. He said nothing of creating half-man-half-woman! There is male and there is female but there is no she-male. On the sixth day he made Adam, and then he made Eve from the rib of Adam. Where is the mention of another sex? This is one dreamed up by the Devil, I tell you.'

'You grasp at straws, Mrs Brown.' I no longer felt at liberty to use her first name considering my rising anger against her. 'Is every creature in this world mentioned in the Bible? No. I assure you it is not. Is a sparrow mentioned? No. What of the badger and the hedgehog? No. Therefore, I tell you, it is evident the Bible does not see fit to list every one of God's creatures. We are all of us God's creatures.'

'Oh, Mrs Harris, how you show ignorance of the book you claim to know so well. Sparrows are very much talked of in the Bible!' I had given Mrs Brown the arrows to shoot me down, and the happiness of being right. 'Have not you read Matthew?' That triumph grew strong in her face until she was alight with it. I was determined to find another way to blow out that light.

'Maybe I am mistaken in that, but I am certain that neither the badger nor hedgehog are there, and that is proof enough! Not every living creature in the world is there in the Bible, but as sure as I am of anything, He made every one of them.'

'Now,' the Justice spoke, but we did not know he spoke to us. 'Now, then. Come forth and explain yourselves.'

Still we argued amongst ourselves. That is until, with a trumpeting voice that reached the farthest corner in a way Shakespeare himself would have been satisfied with, the Justice referred to a piece of Saint Augustine's work that I knew so well.

'Can you find false that great Christian philosopher of all times, Augustine, when he tells us that, when we account for only deformities, we do not see the whole that the Lord has made, the balance of the peculiar with everything else that makes it glorious? I believe that might suit the purpose of the topic I hear you bicker about, a topic that seems to be of the greatest importance to you?'

Our ears alert to the Justice's attention upon us, we stopped our quarrel and faced the man who would make judgement on Mary's fate. I did not imagine he would have any more compassion for Mary's cause than the women. In my experience, a man is singularly unable to place himself in another's man's shoes, let alone in the shoes of one he cannot determine if it be man or woman. It might have been better to have a judgement made by old Mrs Fisher, except that she was born in a past time when she cannot have so great an understanding of the lives of persons today. Though she did seem to have had some sympathy with Mary's plight, she might also yet stand side-by-side with the Aldermen and be as dull-witted as our accuser, Mrs Brown.

'Sir—,' I started, intending to plead my case.

'Madam, I will first hear the one that has brought this problem before me today.' He looked at Mrs Brown, perhaps being used to her bringing many a complaint to his ears.

For the first time that day, Mrs Brown took on a cloak of humbleness. Perhaps for reason of keeping good appearance before the Justice, her husband's acquaintance, as she so often told any that would listen.

'Not I, Sir. Our friend, Mrs Fisher, has come here from London to give us her wisdom on this matter.'

Justice Gape baa-d not unlike an angry sheep.

'Perhaps, rather you might have spared this old woman the long journey if you had come before me sooner.'

'It is no great hardship to come here today, sir.' The old woman spoke slowly with long pauses. She leaned on her stick and none rushed to find her a seat. 'I am often called upon for such matters. It is only the difficulty of this person's cause that presses me to bring this to your attention. I am convinced your wisdom will better allow judgement as to what should be done about it.'

The Justice leaned forward, raised his grey shaggy-cat brows and rested his elbows on his desk. He clasped his hands so they pointed toward us, then set the round softness of his two chins to hang over them.

As he opened his mouth to speak, he was disturbed by a tenuous knock at the open door. With much shuffling and scraping of feet, a man stinking of too long spent in the animal pens came to the desk, neither raising his hat nor even noticing the women seeking counsel with the justice. If we were ticks on a sheep's back he would no doubt have given us more scrutiny. As it was, we were forced to stand aside until his business, none of which could be of the least interest to us, was done. The justice quite forgot we were there.

After the interruption, with neither a by-your-leave nor tilt of his hat, the man trailed mud from his filthy boots back to the door and left. The Justice wrote something in a ledger and took a moment to remember that we formerly had his attention and reluctantly returned to us with a sigh. He studied each of the gathering before speaking to the chosen deputy.

'Mrs Fisher, was it?' Mrs Fisher dipped her head briefly in response. 'Pray, lay before me the problem that has outwitted the wisdom of your many years. What brain-teaser might I find an answer to when age cannot?'

The old woman demanded attention with her deliberate, painful move to Mary's side, even though attention was readily given and need not be asked for. She stretched my patience on the rack of her showmanship, whilst drawing me unwilling into her act. She did not need to bang her stick on the floor as she had earlier, for all eyes could not look elsewhere when she made such a play.

Nevertheless, she banged her stick.

The noise that came through our feet and made every person around her jump. Even the Justice sat up straight.

Mary was perhaps the only one not to answer to the stick's bark. Neither did she show any sign of her earlier fight. She stood broken and ashamed amid the towns-women, who paid her no attention until old Mrs Fisher came to stand before her.

Beneath her eyes the skin plumped out from the sunken area. Her face was not so handsome to see and I could not be comfortable with my part in her undoing. It was I that had further exposed her to injury of honour and spirit. What had I taken from her? What had I left her?

Before Mrs Fisher spoke, and even as she opened her mouth, Mrs Brown was unable to keep her smacking lips together.

'This… person. This…' The woman became stuck on the word as if she could barely say it so changed it to something more tolerable, 'creature… being both male and female, it is not of the natural sexes God saw fit to create for this world. We have uncovered its disguise and demand it be punished for its trickery!'

As so often this day, I clenched my hands by my side to stop myself taking the few steps between myself and Mrs Brown and slapping the smugness from her face. I could not fathom how one such as herself did not see all people as persons. In particular, I did not like the way she talked of Mary as an animal. My voice shook as I began to defend my daughter.

'Mary is as pretty a person as any other in this world. Do not talk of her as if she is not one of God's creatures—'

'And that is a problem to you?' Asked the Justice, surprising me by his interruption. He answered not me but Mrs Brown, but it was not Mrs Brown that answered him.

'It is a problem for the maid who is with-child.' The old woman looked not to the Justice but far away into the rafters of the room as if pondering a problem larger than that of the stars. 'The baby will want for a father, the mother for a husband. This one is neither. It has hid beneath the guise of a sister, but we did reveal its deception and unmask it so it lay naked before us. I am of the mind that if it has the tool to sire a child, then it should not be merely the maker of the child, but should be the father too. It cannot be a sister to its child's mother.'

I could not fault her thinking. I had not had any expectations the Fisher woman would come down on Mary's side, but she had done so, wittingly or unwittingly. If Mary would lief be with Elin and the baby, indeed did believe herself in love with her, then that would answer this predicament with elegance. At that, Mary raised her face and returned Mrs Fisher's study of her. No doubt the woman saw what I saw, and that was hope. Did she understand better than I gave her credit for, or was it merely the simplest answer?

Mrs Brown, standing behind the old woman as if to cut off any escape tried by Mary, quizzed her on her idea.

'Preposterous! You cannot be serious, Mrs Fisher. This... creature, though it did use trickery and guile to conceal itself amongst us has been discovered and now the only place it belongs, if it belongs at all, is on a seat in one of those freak shows that goes from place to place. You cannot suggest it can become what it is not. It has deceived us most darkly and most seriously. We do not want it here. At the very least, it must be cast out, banished from our town!'

'You are mistaken, Mrs Brown,' said the old woman. 'You may think this case most unusual, but in my many years I have witnessed such thing before and I have some knowledge of what I talk about. It may be neither male nor female, but have you not understood it to be a female all these years? Has it not given itself fully to the part its mother has told it and played it very well? I understand you did not know its true nature until it exposed itself. If it was able to disguise itself so completely as a woman in the way it was told to do, then might it be that it can do the same as a man? I am witness to a similar case in London that one such as this may take either part. I do not see what use to banish it when it could equally use that same wit to fill the role that is missing here to great satisfaction of those involved.'

'But that is impossible. We would all know what—'

The Justice, who had heretofore sat quietly and listened as a bystander, his elbows still before him, unclasped his hands and slapped them flat on the dark wood of his table. The flesh of them seemed to spread across its surface as two large unshelled cackling farts in a pan.

'Silence, women. I am not so full of patience to be a bystander in a dispute between the two of you when you have come here to ask for my opinion. If you have a thing to say, then say it to me and let me do what I am here to do.'

Of the women around me, most only half-obeyed his command and half-turned toward him. Mary still looked at Mrs Fisher with interest. I did not have time to wonder why, for the two women, like cocks readying their spurs for a good fight, eyed each other up and down. I imagined Mrs Brown was betrayed by Mrs Fisher coming down on the side of Mary, having brought her here from the city to help cast her out.

'Sir,' said Mrs Brown. 'I bring before you a very serious case. It is one in which all have been deceived, not only those close around it, but every person that has ever laid eyes upon it, for it has tricked us into thinking it a female when all the time it was not.'

'So you have said, Mrs Brown. I see you are quite vexed over this, and you seem to think I have not heard you every other time you have said so.' He lifted his hands to his ears and grabbed the tops sticking out. 'These are working quite well, madam. I have on many occasions talked to your husband and, even living beside the family he has never said a bad word about them. If this one,' he pointed to Mary, 'or any other of them, he gestured toward me and Elin, 'have caused you harm, tell me what it is so I can seek reparation in your name.'

'That one is the worst.' Now Mrs Brown did the pointing, this time at me. Again, I clasped my hands to my side, this time so I would not grab that nasty, pointing finger and make her point it at herself, for she was worse than any other in the town with her malicious tattling. 'It is she that has hidden the creature and pretended it as one of us. It is she who has taken it into our bed-chambers. She has dressed it in petticoats to trick us into letting it in. It is she that has the ear of the Devil, and that creature there is her servant!'

'It is you that is in league with the Devil, Mrs Brown! What harm have I ever done you that you are so against me?' Mary that had before stilled her tongue could hold it no longer.

Mrs Brown turned a deaf ear to Mary and continued to accuse me.

'Perhaps you are right and it is not you the deceiver. Perhaps it is your mother, the Devil's sly servant. She who creeps into an innocent house and casts her wicked spell over a man so that he cannot think of any other, not even his wife!'

If I could have closed my mouth at that time I would not have given her the satisfaction of knowing her barb had pierced me, though I was surprised at her accusation. Surprised, for I had thought nothing more of my visits to the baker shop in the mornings than a piece of hot bread and pleasing conversation. If I had ever thought about it at all, I would not have imagined she knew or cared about my going there when every other person in the town did so as well.

'What—?' I started.

'You! Do not think I am blind to your ways! You steal your way into the baker's shop every morning before daybreak and use your devilry on my husband so his mind is enchanted and he cannot think of anything but you. Then you place a spell over the whole town to take in this creature so that you can send her amongst us, hiding what she is.' If some person had touched my chest right then, I would have fallen over backwards, my legs having lost so much feeling. This woman was so filled with madness against me, each word spat at me with the venom of a snake. 'Now, now, Mrs Harris. Do not play the innocent with us. Your diabolical spell is broken. We see you for what you are!'

I did not have time to answer, for all others in the room spoke together loudly and at once.

'What nonsense, Mrs Brown. She-'

'Are you mad? We are not here to-'

'You dare call Mother a witch! You are of the worst-'

'She has done no such thing-'

'Mrs Brown, you speak out of order.' The last was the Justice. He did not have a hammer, so he picked up his inkpot and banged it down heavily on his desk three times, spilling black liquid over his ledger. When he stopped, he seemed quite taken aback by his actions and examined his desk with sadness, rubbing the polished wood with the tips of his fingers. Then he took up blotting paper and patted his book, talking the while. 'As I understand it, this is not a witch-hunt, but a meeting to decide on the nature of Mrs Harris's child and what we should do about it.'

And then old Mrs Fisher spoke. Where she had spoken with quiet deliberation before, she now raised her voice to a quivering high and rounded on Mrs Brown.

'You bring me here to do your dirty work for you, Mrs Brown. You, too, are a deceiver. What you wish is for me to cast down not only the child, but the mother too, for you cannot keep your man in line. Is this not so? Pretend not that you are here for the town's sake when you are here entirely for your own.' Then she swivelled on her stick to face the Justice more fully. 'Sir, we are not here to point the finger of blame at the fault and flaw of every person in the room, nor even this one's unfortunate family.' Keeping both hands on her stick, she dipped her head toward Mary. 'This woman here would have us blame the mother for keeping her child's nature secret, when it seems she is resolved to do so for reasons of jealousy over her husband. We must hold our thoughts to what is here important, what it is to do with the case and what is not. And that is what we should say to this one, who has lived as a female, but acted as a male. I am of the mind that it has shown willing to do what is right by the maid with-child, and should be obliged to fulfil that part.'

And then she clammed shut her mouth and chewed back any other words, her jaw working on them for some minutes, considering her speech sufficient and needing no elaboration.

Justice Gape replaced his elbows on the table, but clasped his hands together as in prayer. Perhaps he asked God for the answer, and it seemed He did receive one, for his next words were spoken with certainty, as if he had them whispered in his ear.

'Say no more on the matter. I am decided and I will give you the source of my decision so that you may know I have not come to this alone but in the company of great minds. And then I believe someone of you spoke of that wisest of saints, Augustine of Hippo,' he said, forgetting it was himself. 'I am one of his greatest followers and place great importance in the truth of his examination of the Bible. No, do not speak when I am talking!' When Mrs Brown would have said something, he silenced her then returned to what he was saying. 'On the subject of the diversity of persons, I can tell you what he did say. And you will have to pardon me on this, being an ardent follower of that great man, his writings are forever bound in my heart and I am able to quote him at great length.'

He then tilted his head and looked past us at the far wall and quoted from memory.

'*But whoever is anywhere born a man, that is, a rational, mortal animal, no matter what unusual appearance he presents in colour, movement, sound, nor how peculiar he is in some power, part, or quality of his nature, no Christian can doubt that he springs from that one protoplast. We can distinguish the common human nature from that which is peculiar, and therefore wonderful.*' When he had drawn on all he wished from his mind, the Justice's eyes came back to us. 'And now I have told you the source of my decision is in the philosopher's book, The City of God, Book Sixteen, chapter eight. I will tell you my decision as I have made it.'

The man made much of inspecting each of our faces in turn, neither smiling in an encouraging way nor paying any one of us less mind than any other, as if he chose to remember the faces of any that came before him so that he may recall them later if they were to come before him again. I thought he would be the next one to speak, but old Mrs Fisher first said, 'If you know what you will say, perhaps you would be good enough to say it.'

The Justice's throat quivered as he cleared it, then he mumbled as if his mouth was full. 'Yes, perhaps you are right, but if you are come to me for my judgement, you must show patience and hear it.' He stopped chewing on his words and lay his hands back onto the top of the desk. He leaned forward. We leaned forward. 'She,' and he pointed with his whole hand, must become a 'he'. As you have rightly said, Mrs-?' If he had forgotten her name, he was not interested enough to await an answer from Mrs Fisher. 'If a person is male enough to beget a maid with child, then that person must be male enough to be father to that child. And if that is so, then, I say that person must present before a man of God and marry the mother of that said child immediately and without hesitation. And that is what I have to say on that!' Again, he eyed each of us, this time to challenge any of us to say anything against his decision.

Remarkably, none did.

21

Thomas

My daughter I knew well enough, but the man with her was a stranger to me.

Dressed finely in a rather splendid and well-fitting brown justacorps, matching waistcoat and knee-breeches over red stockings, all gently decorated with rust-red ribbon, the man stood tall, back straight, his chin raised in confidence. Wearing a long, dark periwig parted in the middle with curls flowing over his shoulders, he carried his feathered hat beneath his arm. Last, not seen on more than a handful of farming men around the town, his sword hung so I could see its hilt near his waist and the tip lifting the back of his coat behind him.

A most suitable husband for my Elin.

Losing Mary to this man left me more bereft than I could remember. Yet it was right that Elin should have such a fine, upstanding gentleman to marry her. She and the baby deserved to be well cared for.

He was a handsome man.

Just as he had been a handsome woman.

The man, Thomas, dressed in his vampers and kicks, had the semblance of my child, but stood taller and more confident.

The man, Thomas, that once was Mary, embraced Elin with the intimacy of a suitor having won her heart in a joust when once he was forbidden to enter the tournament; of being previously denied to hold her hand but now anticipated an eternity of kisses.

Thomas let go of Elin and came to me, took my shoulders and looked deep into my eyes. His own cornflower eyes were beautiful. I had never noticed how long were his lashes before, but now they appeared longer.

'You are a handsome man,' I said.

Yet he was also the most beloved child I had reared as a castaway, unwanted by either mother or father.

And when he spoke, his voice was the most familiar of all things. In it lived on the daughter I had lost, taken by the son I had gained. The change was more than a change in habit, though that in itself marked a difference in my perception and understanding of her... him.

'Do not grieve for me, Mother, for though I am Thomas I am Mary as well. Perhaps more so. She will always and ever be the greatest part of who I have been and so who I am.'

It was not as if I could not understand the bodily differences, for that had been our burden for more years, as many as I could remember. Living with it had been our nature and our secret. Now Mary was no longer boxed in by that secret. Her discovery had released her to choose not only which sex to live as, but the character she would live it as. That she chose to be male only happened along at the same time as she was ordered to do so, to fulfil her role as husband and father and provide for the child she sired.

I noted of myself I still did not call her 'him' and would take a good deal of time to become used to doing so. Faster to become accustomed to were the gentlemanly traits she had so easily acquired, which tended toward the softer side of society. Somehow what had made her the sweetest, the kindest, the most affable of women also gave the man she had become the mannerisms of higher society and of a more complex disposition. Imagining her to be the tailor she would become in London was not beyond mine or any other person's capability.

The two of them would, I was certain, do well for themselves in the city, where none but Mrs Fisher knew the story of Mary Jewett - now Thomas Jewett - and they would have every opportunity to rear their child in privacy. Privacy, not secrecy. The difference was one of choice, a quite dissimilar notion.

If only it were so simple for myself. What if, like... Thomas, I could show my own true nature without judgement upon me? But why would I? I had no reason to expose myself. But if I did, perhaps

I too might find happiness and live unconcealed and without a veil of secrecy. Yet I had lived this way too long to change myself and no longer had the desire to as once I did.

'I will come to London a full fourteen-night and no later than a sennight before your lying-in unless you send for me before.'

I, too, embraced Elin when she came into my arms. She stood some distance away and leaned in, holding my shoulders long and tight to allow for the growing mound of her baby until I did wonder if she would squeeze the last breath from me. Instead I held her with equal tightness while our tears cleared sorrow from our hearts to allow us to go our two separate ways.

Elin nodded into my shoulder, sniffled and said, 'I will look to that day with the greatest anticipation, Mother.' When I opened my eyes, Thomas wore wariness as strangely as his new clothes. I blinked the mistiness from my eyes and Elin pulled back, her face flushed not with sadness but with happiness and child-bearing. 'We shall not be strangers,' she said. With the greatest effort I returned her smile. A half-smile was all I could muster.

But it was Thomas that now took my attention.

Thomas.

The twin of my daughter, he seemed to have fast become comfortable with having cut short his hair and replaced it with the periwig. In fact, he confided that he felt quite released wearing the loose curls around his shoulder as was the mode in town. Neither did he seem out of sorts wearing Widow Hopkins' dead husband's clothes that someone had the thinking to fetch from the good woman for a few shillings when they remembered his shape and size must be a good fit for Mary's. And when she put them on, it seemed she became the man she wished to be. In brown breeches, most often used for attending town meetings and other such gatherings, Thomas presented himself as a fine young man ready for the city. Indeed, that was a thing Mary had often talked of with Elin of late, and now they two would go together as an adventure!

Thomas did not seem as I had expected him to be before setting off on a quest for his dreams. There was more concern there than happiness. His next warm words confirmed it was for me and my own possible plight.

'Will they forgive you, Mother? Do they still turn from you?'

'Do not be so apprehensive, Ma- Thomas.' If I ever remembered his new name, I would be grateful to the Lord for his assistance in this. 'I am sure my earlier suffering and torment will prove founded on baseless fears. There are some that pay no mind to such matters and some that dwell out of town that will not be concerned with the tattle that will surely come from this. And for those that pay more mind, the memory of a person might be long, but I shall seek forgiveness wherever any will give it and, in time, perhaps I will gain back my reputation.'

'If they do not forgive you, will you forgive me? I did not intend this.'

I took his hand in mine, remembering so often doing so with the same hand on another person, and rubbed the top of it with my own. His hand was as soft as it had ever been. With no thought to whether it might now be the wrong thing to do, I took his hand and placed it high on my chest. 'My heart will ever be with you, my child, and no change of clothes and no distance will make it otherwise. I will not have you go without an embrace from you, for I do not know when you will come again and I cannot wait that long.'

We closed the gap and held each other tight. When I closed my eyes, the warm smell of lavender was as it always was and he did feel the same. My Mary stood there, separated from me by only some few thin pieces of fabric, the only difference being in the way they were sewn together.

Then we separated and our hands found each other briefly before losing each other at the fingertips. He turned and took Elin's hand and aided her up the steps of the rattler. They were the only customers and Elin placed herself facing forward and Thomas sat facing back, both next to the nearest windows. I took the hands they held out to me through the window, one in each of my own, and worked hard not to spill more tears and failed.

'Forgive me if I am out of line, Mother, but I did ask Judith if she will assist you in your work and she has said yes. She will do all I ever did for you and perhaps better.' He smiled a true smile then and my heart lurched. I already ached for his leaving. And Elin. But it was Mary's strength and wit that had always helped me through the difficult times. Judith was but a child, but at her age Mary had shown wisdom greater than her years and had been the perfect midwife's assistant. I must still my misgivings and give her opportunity to show herself. I sighed. Except for her plaiting, she was not a quick learner. 'She will do, Mother. Let her show you.'

'I will, Mary.' Thinking of her in the past, I forgot to use her new name. She did not set me right. 'And I trust you will stay safe and will write to me once you are settled there and tell me how goes your life in London?'

The coachman came outside from the Peahen Inn near which he had stopped his horses. He set down his tankard on an oak table nearby the open door, filled with other such empty vessels, and strode across to the coach. Placing one foot on the front-step, in one bound he was aboard and in the coachman's seat. 'Ho,' he said. Having had his drink, he was ready to go. His voice was long and stretched-out in the coachman's calling to his horses. 'To London and away.' He flicked his whip in the air behind the horses' ears and away they galloped, the hands of Thomas and Elin slipping from mine as they went out of reach. Both waved until they disappeared from sight. I waved back until I could no longer see them, then my arms dropped heavily to my sides. I turned full of sorrow I should not see them again for some good while, and went home my eyes blind to all but memories in my mind.

Judith came home a full half hour earlier than the curfew bell. Before she came in the door, having no clients to see to, I had busied myself by sweeping the floor, scrubbing the doorstep, brushing down the curtains and preparing the evening meal. Seeing to the needs of the house gave me more than enough time to ponder on the change of Mary to Thomas and the nature of the difference and the sameness of the two.

And that brought me round to pondering that of my own nature.

In truth, Mary's tale was not so different than my own. Leastways, not until now. But we did not wholly share our story.

My reasoning had been sound as had been my mother's. It was my mother's wisdom that had guided me the last one and twenty years, just as it had guided me nigh on thirty years before that. If I had heard my mother's warning once, I had heard it often, indeed no less often than Mary. I too had been condemned to keep the secret. I too was warned to take care how I should be seen. I, too, had slept in the bed with my sisters. But I was never filled with a young lover's lusty spirit with them, nor did I ever leave the role my mother did for my safe-keeping instruct me in.

As well, I did heed my mother closely when she said I should never try to take myself a husband. It was for two-fold reasons I obeyed her. The first was for my mother, that I should not be discovered, for the memory of Aunt Biddy was clear enough in all of us that I would never test a man's love in that way. The second was that I was never inclined to take to any suitor that presented himself, and it was not for the lack of them. In truth, I was myself considered to be a handsome woman when I came of age and was not without the attentions of a young man or two.

But never did I wish or allow intimacy with any of them.

It was easier to pretend disinterest in marriage altogether.

Yet it was not that my heart was never captured. To say that was so would be to deny the one I dreamed of, one over whom I was in raptures, one who engaged my senses. It would be another falsehood.

Still now, I remembered her, how we walked together. How, as we went to church on Sunday, we talked often of worldly things as if we were sisters. But never did I tremble when I sat with my sisters as I did when I sat with her. Never did my heart sing to me as it did when the warmth of her legs through her petticoats pressed close to mine on the church pew. And I was not compelled to reach out and caress my sisters or seek them out as I sought her very soul deep within her eyes.

Sadly, I never did find it, for it was never there for me. She was not made as I.

I often told her that I loved her, and allowed her to believe my tenderness for her was the sweetest friendship. As indeed it was, but it was more too. When the Lord God Almighty took her to sit beside him, I cried for the loss of my dear companion and that I would never find that sweet love again in any other person. I did not. Nor did I seek it. The heartache of losing her to the sickness was more than I could ever again bear.

In the art of midwifery I learned at my mother's side I found I had a gift. In it, I soon gained a reputation as one that had more live births than ill, and my care before and after the lying-in was second to none others in the town. It was into my art, then, that I took my grieving and used it to bring life into the world.

My sister was one that chose my services over those of our mother. So tight was the secret our mother made me keep that even she, close as we had been in our childhood years, did not know it. And for that reason, when the infant Mary later began to change, she did not know how she belittled me when she belittled her child.

'Take it. It is an abomination as was our mother's sister. Take it and be rid of it.' She thrust the small body into my hands. When I would not, she said, 'I will have none of it. I will not watch it suffer the taunts of the town until it is forced to turn off its own life in order to avoid further anguish. Better to let it die quickly than let it live only to die at its own hand.'

Even though I persuaded her against action that day, it only delayed her baby's fate. It was surely by the grace of God that I came across her husband following her wishes some months later, so the infant Mary came to be with the one person in the world that might understand and save her. And so we two, Mary and me, found a place together. And in her coming to me, I too was saved, for God had sent her to me to heal my broken heart. And then, not satisfied with his good work, he sent me two more, though not formed in the same mould, that were to bring me great joy.

Mary, then Elin, then Judith. I was blessed with them all. And now two were gone.

By that time, the iron door-latch lifted with a clunk, and Judith came in from the street and ran to embrace me, with 'Are they gone?'

'Boots!' I said, placing my fists on my waist and pretending a scold.

My single voice sounded strange where before there had been three, but I would be used to it given time.

I had done my thinking.

Would I reveal my secret?

It was not in my heart to do so. My path was otherwise. If my life's task was to raise my rescued children, give them a decent and goodly life and help them find their own path, then in that I had succeeded with two on their way to make their happiness in the city. But the task was not yet finished. And for the last one, Judith, I would be her mother. She needed only that and no other. For that reason, I would take my secret with me to my grave, for I did not wish to be any different..

'They would have me say farewell to you, and bring you to London if ever I go that way. I am sure we shall find reason a-plenty when the baby comes.' I smiled. I was certain there would be many reasons to travel to the city, more now than ever before. I wiped my hands on my skirt and smiled at my last child. 'Shall we take some supper?'

The End

For God, the Creator of all, knows where and when each thing ought to be, or to have been created, because He sees the similarities and the diversities, which can contribute to the beauty of the whole. But he who cannot see the whole is offended by the deformity of the part, because he is blind to that which balances it, and to which it belongs.

-Saint Aurelius Augustine (Bishop of Hippo) 354-430 AD

Glossary

Stone-horse water (or stone horse dung water)
Liquid from the dung of an uncastrated stallion, believed to bring on pregnancy and also used to alleviate after-pains

Caudle
A thick, sweetened drink/gruel for the sick, invalids or, here, to help with pain relief during childbirth as well as a restorative after. Often thickened with egg yolk, wheat starch or breadcrumbs and often dosed with alcohol (wine or ale), it might be flavoured with ginger (or perhaps other spices) and sultanas.

Crackling fart
Hen's egg

In her throes (originally spelt 'throws')
Having birth contractions

Travels
From *The Midwives Book* (1671) written by 17th century midwife, Jane Sharp. She refers to 'travels' and 'throws' in the birth process:

> *A Child may be sometimes very weak, yet not dead, take heed you do not force delivery in such occasions till you be sure it is time, for children may be sick and faint in their Mothers*

bellies. But to prevent danger, burn half a pint of white-wine adding no Spice to it, but half an ounce of Cinnamon and drink it off: if your Travel and throws come upon you, be sure it is dead; but if it be but sick and weak, it will refresh it and strengthen it.

It's likely, but uncertain, whether the exact meaning is the modern meaning of 'trevails.'

Common shore

Sewer. Usually where not only human and animal waste goes, but also the animal blood, entrails and other animal remains from the butchers as well as lye from soap-making and ingredients used in the leather-making process etc.

Vaspers and kicks

Stockings and breeches

Pudding hat

Cap or material round a young child's head to prevent bumps and bruises from falling and banging into things.

Justacorps or justaucorps

Knee-length coat worn with waistcoat and tighter knee-breeches than the previous petticoat (or rhinegraves) versions and stockings. The coat, waistcoat and breeches thought to be the forerunner of the three-piece suit.

Acknowledgements

A book is never a book without some thank-yous to the people who have supported the author through the long time of writing it and the longer time (for me at least) of editing it. This book is no different. There are some very special people who've been there for me during this last time, and I hope I remember everyone.

First, because she has been there throughout each and every day, and because she is one of my biggest supporters, advisors, inspirors, chivviers and because she never ceases to amaze me with her wisdom and loyalty, my daughter Rhianna. Thank you, my dear, for everything.

My writing buddy of more than ten years, Tim Savage, has helped and advised me on all manner of things, not least with feedback about this story and formatting the book. Indeed, this last year, we've taken a shared writing interest a step further to begin a writing collaboration for fun. Thank you for being a good friend, lifting me up when I struggled, even when you were yourself also being tested by life.

I am also grateful to the gems of beta readers who agreed to read *The Midnight Midwife*, in no particular order: Alice Noel-Johnson; Chandra Lahiri; Shirley Sakovits; Teresa Broderick; Andrea Stoeckel; Judi Imperato; Donna Micco; Emma Davis.

I appreciate that, for some, a few of the issues covered were uncomfortable, and so I especially appreciate those that read it to the end. I was struck by their honesty and frankness. Thank you for agreeing to read and give feedback. Thank you also for catching the typos that nearly fell through the net.

As always, thanks to my family and friends for being there. You are the pillars that support my world around me.

About Annelisa Christensen

Annelisa Christensen was born in Sussex, majored in psychology at the University of Stirling in Scotland, then returned to the south of England to partner in a successful fashion company with her childhood friend, Julia, creating Inca-inspired designs. They dissolved 'Macchu Picchu' when their children came along a few years later.

Although, ever since her first story at aged eight, she has filled several suitcases of hand- and type-written writing experiments, it wasn't until 2007 she was able to finally add her first novel to them. This she did as a single mother of four (two with severe OCD), and while working as a laboratory technician in the school in which she was Head Girl twenty years earlier.

Then, Madam Serendipity launched Annelisa onto a course of her writing career she would never have otherwise considered.

Through an online auction win, she placed into the author's hands some disbound pages of a 300-year-old trial. Annelisa fell in love with the defendant, a bold and sassy seventeenth century midwife, Elizabeth Cellier, falsely accused of treason during the English Restoration period, and had to find out more about this woman. So began some deep research into Cellier's life. And the more Annelisa discovered about this forward-thinking woman, the stronger her desire to share her story. After several years, her labour of love gave birth to the award-winning *The Popish Midwife*.

It didn't stop there. Drawn inexorably into this lesser-known era of plague, treason and burning cities and, in particular, toward the midwives, a remarkable group of strong women surviving in that world, Christensen embraced her destiny to share their stories in a series succinctly called *Seventeenth Century Midwives*.

Christensen chose the second tale of the series, *The Ghost Midwife*, because it portrays a particular issue dealt with by midwives throughout the ages, but which drew popular attention through several disturbing cases towards the end of the 17th century. The issue is that of illegitimate and unwanted infants, which midwives were often paid by the parish to keep. Mistress Atkins was such a midwife. After her death, she came back to haunt the servants of Rotten Row and to warn others not to do as she did. The novella is based on a 1680 ballad.

The third tale, *The Midnight Midwife*, is also based on a seventeenth century ballad. This one is set in the market town of St. Albans, just north of London. Annelisa uses the story to focus on another issue relevant to midwives of the time: the role of women in the birth-chamber and the exclusion of men from it. 21 years ago, when adopting an unwanted infant, a mother made a choice. Now, her daughter lives a life she never wanted and her mother is forced to reflect she may have made the wrong choice.

The French Midwife is the fourth book in the series and, like *The Popish Midwife*, is a deeper novel based on extended research. Annelisa discovered this midwife whilst researching Elizabeth Cellier, because she was also sometimes referred to as 'The Popish

Midwife.' Though she came to England as a huguenot (Protestant), Marie Des Ormeaux (also known as Mary Hobry) became a Catholic through marriage, a marriage which was ultimately to be the death of her. In 1688, Marie faced trial for the murder of her husband Denis. Annelisa quickly realised this was the story of love gone bad, the story of a husband's abuse and a woman pushed too far. Self defence or revenge? That, you will have to decide for yourself.

Please support the Author

Other readers rely on reviews to know whether or not a book would be a suitable/enjoyable read for themselves. Please leave a line or two to let others know what you think with a review on Amazon, Goodreads and any other reading place you might hang out. Annelisa also likes to hear what you think and can be found online:

- Author website
  http://www.annelisachristensen.com

- Twitter @Alpha_Annelisa

- Instagram @Alpha_Annelisa

- Blog: Script Alchemy
  www.scriptalchemy.com

- Facebook
  www.facebook.com/ScriptAlchemy

- Goodreads
  www.goodreads.com/author/show/15489090.Annelisa_Christensen

- Historical Novel Society
  historicalnovelsociety.org/directory/annelisa-christensen

  *Join her mailing list on any of the above sites

A preview from

The Popish Midwife

First in the *Seventeenth Century Midwives* series

'Come, Madam Cellier, are you not delighted to see me? I warned you I would return.'

Waller was ten years my junior and surprisingly strong for his lesser stature. With very little effort, he dragged me back to the kitchen, where Dowdal leaned against the wall beside the door to the back of the house as yet unseen. Perhaps they did not see him because he held no importance for them. I watched as he slipped away out the door, before the last of Waller's men were even in the room. If only I had left more swiftly, I may have been far away by now.

My children must be somewhere nearby, though they were quiet and did not draw scrutiny to themselves. Perhaps they smelt the wickedness of the Priest-catcher as he approached or sensed the urgency of Dowdal's warning and hid away, else they had preceded Dowdal out of the door. With hope, the last. Either way, not even little Maggie, who rarely stayed quiet, could be heard, for which I could only release my breath in a slow sigh of relief.

'I would gladly supply invited guests with mulled sac or cider, yet must admit to having none to sweeten you with. I fear we midwives drink so much ourselves, we have little left over for entertaining.' My intuition told me I should play the female card, for he saw himself as a man of honour though he was not.

'Do not fret, Madam Cellier, we will make our own entertainment. Perhaps you have superstitious blood we might drink instead?' Waller's men laughed at his supposed wit, casting aspersions on the red wine used in communion. The men all carried swords at their sides, so I swallowed the quip about communion blood running stronger than his own to the King.

'I would be delighted if you would have wine and wafer with me, Sir Waller, but I think you do not have the taste for it.'

'And I would be delighted if you would stand aside while we did the work we came to do but fear you would rather hinder me in the path of justice.'

'I would stand aside if I knew what side to stand on,' I said.

'You stand on the wrong side, Madam Cellier,' he responded. 'You chose the wrong side when you chose to stand on the side of the Devil.' Sir Waller was not amused by my having a voice, and took amusement in degrading me.

'What causes you to think that? I walk with God, and He walks with me.'

The sound of them searching the children's bedchamber and ours broke our conversation, and gave me a fervent wish to discover what they were doing. Even in this room where we stood, as before, his men ransacked the same cupboards and drawers they had searched previously, but this time also lifted and moved the cupboards to look behind, and stamped on the wood planks, perhaps hoping to find a secret hole where treasonable things were hidden.

Since I did not know where anything was hidden, I could not react if they came close. In that, the Judas serpent was right. My innocence might save me.

'You are mistaken, madam. He walks with true believers, not with those of superstitious beliefs. You have chosen the Popish ways, and they are against the King's rules and against the King himself. We have testimony that you hide proof of your traitorousness in this house, and we will find them. Your friend, Dangerfield, has told us all we need know of your scheme, and he has revealed that he has seen the proof here. Admit your scheme now, and we will be lighter on you.'

'Who is this Dangerfield? I know him not.'

'You tell me you do not know one who has lived under your very roof with you? This I cannot believe!'

'I know of no Dangerfield,' I insisted.

'Perhaps you know of him by the name of Captain Thomas Willoughby?' he said, then smiled when he saw my understanding grow.

'I know Willoughby, but not Dangerfield,' I reiterated.

'Do not play this game with me, Madam. You must know they are one and the same.' We walked up the stairs whilst we talked. Through the open door to the children's bedchamber, I watched as a man pulled the bed linen off their bed and then lifted the mattress to find nothing beneath. Then he took his knife and slashed the mattresses open and pulled the horse hair out.

'I did not know that,' I said, 'but I have no scheme to tell you.'

'We know the scheme, but if you will save yourself you must admit to it now.'

'Would you have me lie to save myself? '

'No, I would have you tell the truth and admit your plan to kill the King to aid the Duke.'

I followed Waller back down the stairs to the kitchen. I answered to his back. The kitchen was being ransacked.

'I am a loyal subject to both King and Duke and would only protect them with all the honesty and goodness in me.'

As I said this, a man stopped lifting lids off my pewter pans and raised the lid of the butter tub. When he then lifted the larger rice tub lid, I saw he would search the other food tubs too, and called out to him, 'Keep your dirty hands out of my food,' which was a mistake, for immediately he looked at Sir Waller and received a nod of agreement. He plunged his hand deep into the wood barrel right up to his elbow. Rice spilled on the floor as he moved his searching hand inside. I thought he would turn the whole full tub onto the floor.

'Check the other tubs!' said Sir Waller.

They did not take long to find the papers Willoughby or,

rather, this man Dangerfield, gave me to hide and that Anne had hidden in the barrel of flour.

'Here is treason!' Triumphantly, the man, his arm surrounded by a cloud of white meal, held the papers high in the air. "Tis hid in the meal tub!'…

Printed in Great Britain
by Amazon

34307726R00121